JOSSEY-BASS TEACHER

Jossey-Bass Teacher provides educators with practical knowledge and tools to create a positive and lifelong impact on student learning. We offer classroom-tested and research-based teaching resources for a variety of grade levels and subject areas. Whether you are an aspiring, new, or veteran teacher, we want to help you make every teaching day your best.

From ready-to-use classroom activities to the latest teaching framework, our value-packed books provide insightful, practical, and comprehensive materials on the topics that matter most to K–12 teachers. We hope to become your trusted source for the best ideas from the most experienced and respected experts in the field.

The Second City Guide to Improv in the Classroom

USING IMPROVISATION TO TEACH SKILLS AND BOOST LEARNING

Katherine S. McKnight
and
Mary Scruggs

JOSSEY-BASS
A Wiley Imprint
www.josseybass.com

Published by Jossey-Bass
A Wiley Imprint
989 Market Street, San Francisco, CA 94103-1741—www.josseybass.com

Jossey-Bass books and products are available through most bookstores. To contact Jossey-Bass directly call our Customer Care Department within the U.S. at 800-956-7739, outside the U.S. at 317-572-3986, or fax 317-572-4002.

Jossey-Bass also publishes its books in a variety of electronic formats. Some content that appears in print may not be available in electronic books.

Library of Congress Cataloging-in-Publication Data

McKnight, Katherine S. (Katherine Siewert)
    The Second City guide to improv in the classroom : using improvisation to teach skills and boost learning grades K–12 / Katherine S. McKnight and Mary Scruggs.
        p.   cm.
    Includes index.
    ISBN 978-0-7879-9650-5 (paper)
        1. Creative teaching.   2. Education—Experimental methods.   3. Active learning.   4. Improvisation (Acting)   I. Scruggs, Mary.   II. Second City (Theater company)   III. Title.
    LB1027.3.M39   2008
    371.39—dc22

                                                                                          2007047365

FIRST EDITION
PB Printing   10 9 8 7 6 5 4 3 2

ABOUT THIS BOOK

This book is the result of the educational programming offered by The Second City Training Centers in Chicago and Toronto. The mission of Second City's Education Program is to provide teachers with training, curriculum development, and performance programs that have a lasting impact on student learning. These programs explore and expand upon the techniques and training methods developed by The Second City instructors, actors, and directors, and the program staff collaborates with the educational community to develop curriculum that reaches across content areas in the classroom and beyond.

Second City's Education Program has impacted thousands of students and teachers who have embraced improvisation as a dynamic tool for teaching and learning and has prompted teachers to ask for a book that helps them incorporate improv in the classroom. This book was created to fulfill that need. It features dozens of lessons across the content areas written by teachers who have participated in Second City's "Improvisation for Creative Pedagogy" workshops. The improvisation exercises included in this book are explained and described in classroom contexts. The book also provides detailed information on brain research and current learning theory, as the authors explore the critical connections between improvisation and classroom learning.

ABOUT THE AUTHORS

Katherine S. McKnight, Ph.D., has been a literacy educator for over 16 years. A former high school English teacher, she currently works as associate professor of Secondary Education at National-Louis University. She also trains educators regularly as a professional development consultant for the National Council of Teachers of English. Katie publishes regularly in professional journals and is a frequent presenter at education conferences. Her previous books include *Teaching Writing in the Inclusive Classroom: Strategies and Skills for All Students* (coauthored with Roger Passman) and *Teaching the Classics in the Inclusive Classroom: Reader Response Activities to Engage All Learners* (coauthored with Bradley Berlage). Both are published by Jossey-Bass.

Mary Scruggs is Head of Writing and Education Programs at The Second City Training Centers in Chicago. She codeveloped Second City's "Improvisation for Creative Pedagogy" program, which has taught elementary and secondary teachers about the power of improvisation as an engaging teaching and learning tool for the classroom.

In addition to Mary's work in education, she is also a nationally acclaimed playwright whose work has been produced in several Chicago theaters. Her work includes *The Fairy Trials*, a series of plays based on classic fairy tales designed to teach the public about their court system. Mary coauthored *Process: An Improviser's Journey* with Michael Gellman (Northwestern University Press, 2008).

To our mother, who showed us the lessons in play, and our father, who showed us the play in lessons.

Katie dedicates this book to Jim, Ellie, and Colin, who bring joy to my life.

Mary dedicates this book to Richard, William, and the whole cast of characters we've created together.

CONTENTS

ACKNOWLEDGMENTS

We started the journey of this book with the idea of play, and it is fitting for us to come back to what we all first knew: play. When we were little girls, sharing a bedroom that had two Sears canopy beds with pink polyester bedding, the beds became our first stages as we presented performances for each other, the canopy frames and bedding making a perfect curtained proscenium arch. Our canopy beds are long gone, but we have found plenty of new stages. We never forgot how to play—and we never forgot that to play is to learn.

It was four years ago that we discussed our ideas about improvisation as a pedagogical tool for the classroom with Rob Chambers and Anne Libera from the Second City Training Center. Rob and Anne encouraged us to make the connections that we needed to convince the educational community that this pedagogical approach is engaging as students explore content areas in curriculum, specifically in literacy. The many teachers who participated in the educational programs at the Second City offered advice, insights, suggestions, and valuable critiques that allowed us to draw even deeper connections between improvisation and teaching and learning. We are grateful for their professional commitment to teach our children and their contributions to this work.

Speaking of the contributions of educators, there are a few that we would like to specifically recognize. Katy Smith added important insights to the lessons and ideas in this book. Her sense of humor, keen analysis, and love for drama are appreciated. Brad Berlage also needs to be recognized for his shared understanding of application of improvisation to the teaching of mathematics. Roger Passman also assisted us in harvesting data as we examined connections between improvisation and teaching and learning. We would also like to thank the many teachers and students who welcomed us into their classrooms.

Our friends at Jossey-Bass were always helpful and supportive throughout the creative process of this book. Margie McAneny, our editor, guided this book from conception to fruition. Julia Parmer and Lesley Iura always provided guidance. We are also grateful for our production editor, Justin Frahm, for his keen sense of humor and professional expertise during the final phase of this book.

Katie would also like to thank her Second City classmates and teachers as she developed a deeper and more intimate understanding of improvisation as an art form.

Mary would like to acknowledge her husband, Richard, and her son, William, whose love and support give her the strength to face so many challenges. Also, Mary would like to thank her colleagues at the Second City for their creativity, insights, and knowledge.

Katie would like to acknowledge her family, Jim, Ellie, and Colin, whose patient understanding is appreciated when she needs to go to "the tower" to write.

Our mom, Patricia Siewert, a recently retired public school teacher of thirty-four years, has been supportive of us as we hammered out our ideas for this book. She often made connections with English language learners, her area of expertise, and was a wonderful "roadie" companion on our trips to various educational conferences as we spread the word about improvisation and the connections to teaching and learning.

Finally, we would like to acknowledge our father, Raymond Siewert (1932–1989), who taught us not only how to play but the value of creative expression. His lifelong love of writing and performing found many outlets: he performed in community theater and a few commercials, he wrote mysteries, he taught public speaking to business professionals, and he knew how to tell a great story. Through his example and his enthusiastic support of our creative endeavors, we understood that creative play deepens our understanding of ourselves and brings us closer to each other.

It Begins with Play

It all begins with the concept of play.

When we think of play, it is often associated with small children in preschool classrooms—building with blocks, dressing up, holding tea parties with stuffed animal guests, playing house, recreating stories, acting out vocations such as firefighter, police officer, grocery store cashier. But as students progress through school, play makes way for the more important business of learning core subjects: reading, writing, and arithmetic. If play is given any time, it is as a break from hard work. Play must be earned and is quickly withheld as a consequence of not completing enough real work.

The famous early childhood educator Maria Montessori had different ideas about play. She argued that play was work; it is the work of children and is central to child development. According to Montessori, children learn best when they are active, and therefore they should have a variety of play experiences in the content areas of mathematics, language, and science as well as social relations with peers. Play links sensory-motor, cognitive, and social emotional experiences. Play is the optimal setting for brain development. Play fully develops the complex and integrated brain, so essential for learning throughout childhood and adulthood. In short, play forms the foundation for a fulfilling life.

MONTESSORI'S CONNECTION BETWEEN PLAY AND LEARNING

To further examine the connections between play and learning, let's look at Montessori's notions (1995) about play. Montessori defined the essential dimensions of play as:

- Being voluntary, enjoyable, purposeful, and spontaneous
- Expanding creativity by using problem-solving skills, social skills, language skills, and physical skills
- Helping to expand on new ideas
- Supporting the child in adapting socially
- Serving to thwart emotional problems

From this list of essential dimensions of play, we can easily discern that play is a conduit for learning.

SPOLIN'S CONNECTION BETWEEN PLAY AND LEARNING

Montessori's ideas about play and learning are echoed in the work (1986) of Viola Spolin. She was a foundational creative theorist for what we now refer to as improvisation, a highly structured form of theater based on games. Like Montessori, Spolin argued the merits of play for learning and social interaction among peers. Originally trained as a settlement worker and having studied at Neva Boyd's Group Work School in Chicago, Spolin was heavily influenced by her mentor's innovative teaching, which promoted social interaction. Spolin created theater games with a powerful commitment to the idea that play develops spontaneity and communication within an ensemble of players, communication with the audience (who are themselves part of the game), and problem-solving skills. She asserted that learning the games is a process of problem solving, not a process of students receiving information from a teacher. Through theater games, children learn how to play and develop skills in focus, concentration, self-expression, creativity, problem solving, and more.

In Spolin's view, play:

- Develops and demands focus that prompts our physical and mental state to merge.
- Creates a game having a specific problem to be solved. Players engage intuitive energy through improvisation and develop problem-solving skills.
- Prompts the merging of action and thought to solve a problem.

Throughout this book, we discuss the many teaching and learning connections to improvisation theater games. Without doubt, there are a great many more to be discovered. We think that Spolin summarized it best: "Theater games are a process applicable to any field, discipline, or subject matter which creates a place where full participation, communication, and transformation can take place" (1974).

WHAT HAS HAPPENED TO PLAY?

If play is the conduit for learning, what happens after preschool? Play is often lost in the educational agendas, and what preschoolers think of as play gets split into two categories: "recess" and the more serious, academic-sounding "fine arts," which includes visual arts, music, and drama. Most states have laws mandating recess and physical education, acknowledging that children need this kind of play for good health. But the fine arts rarely receive such support. Because fine arts are often misperceived as "soft" subjects, they are often the first to be sacrificed when budgets are tight. In this volume, we present ample evidence to support the assertion that this utter disregard for the arts is misguided, because the arts are central to the proper development of cognitive and social skills.

This disregard for the importance of the arts in our lives isn't restricted to children. People of all ages have lost their connection to the arts, because most consume far more art than they create. A century ago, people had more opportunities to sing together than listen to professional musicians, more opportunities to tell stories than watch them, more opportunities to create something visually pleasing such as a quilt or a woodcarving than purchase one. In this digitized age, we buy our music, we buy our stories, we buy our images. We have fewer occasions for simple artistic expression and therefore fewer experiences of the authentic communication that comes from participation in the arts. As a result, we are drifting farther and farther away from one of our most essential needs as human beings: to create.

Like any field of knowledge, the arts are a way to understand ourselves and our world. Like any discipline, be it biology, composition, or geometry, the arts have rules and rigor that a participant must engage in and master in order to be successful. All of the arts require content knowledge; discipline; practice; collaboration; and critical, analytical, intuitive, and creative-thinking skills.

Theater is no different from any of the other arts, and improvisation is a specific discipline within the broader context of theater study. At its core, improvisation taps into our deepest, most elemental urges: the desire to play, pretend, and connect. Theater games satisfy our desire to make real what exists in our imagination, whether what we imagine is a fantastic spaceship, or the memory of our grandmother's smile, or the sensation of walking through freshly fallen snow. Improvisation quells a longing we all harbor: to gather round the fire at nightfall and share our experiences. The art form is as old as humanity; it has roots in the first time someone tried to communicate through acting out, rather than explaining, something that happened.

Improvisation also develops our ability to create and share information. One of Spolin's objectives in developing her theater games was to help children develop the skills necessary to perform scripted material. Her son, Paul Sills, the creator of Story Theater and the first director of The Second City, used his mother's work as a foundation for creating content, leading to his own exciting and innovative work in the theater.

In the five decades since Sills directed his first show for The Second City, improvisation has become virtually synonymous with spontaneous, cutting-edge comedy. In Chicago alone, many theaters and schools of improvisation have sprouted up and flourished alongside Second City, most notably iO Theater, founded by Second City alumnus Del Close and Charna Halpern, and the Annoyance Theater, founded by Second City alumnus Mick Napier. As a result, the art form of improvisation has grown since Spolin, with new games and new philosophies and new ideas. Spolin, who encouraged growth, said, "Theatre techniques are far from sacred. Styles in theater change radically with the passing of years, for the techniques of theater are the techniques of communicating. The actuality of the communication is far more important than the method used. Methods alter to meet the needs of time and place" (Spolin, 1999, p. 14).

It is in this spirit that Second City embarked on bringing improvisation into the classroom.

WHY IMPROVISATION WORKS IN THE CLASSROOM

As we have discussed, the arts take their place among all academic disciplines governed by rules and rigor. Meaningful study of improvisation requires:

- Content knowledge
- Discipline
- Collaboration
- Social interaction
- Practice
- Critical thinking skills
- Analytical thinking skills

- Intuitive thinking skills

- Creative thinking skills

Aren't these the kinds of skills that we need to teach in schools so that students can become active participants in our democratic society?

Improvisation is an ideal pedagogical strategy for teaching and learning because it has both inherent structure and flexibility. The inherent structure stems from the rules of each game and the process of problem solving that players must apply to achieve a satisfying experience in playing the game. Flexibility stems from simplicity; no props, scenery, costumes, lighting are required. The players create everything that is needed from their own imagination.

It is this paradoxical nature that makes improvisation a useful tool for developing excellent writers, actors, and thinkers. In this stripped-down, bare-bones dramatic form, there is no limit to what the imagination can conjure into being; yet the form demands specificity, clarity, and logic if it is to be meaningful to the audience. The students are the authors, actors, and audience of work that melds body, voice, and mind through the shared experiences of the players on stage.

THE SECOND CITY CONNECTION

For nearly fifty years, The Second City did not have an ongoing presence in the educational community. Four years ago, we decided to change that. The Second City already had in place a very successful training center with a full range of classes for adults as well as children. Over the years, individual educators had asked us to develop short workshops for their students, but we wanted to do more. Through our experience working with adults as well as children, we knew that the study of improvisation could transform how people interact with the world around them.

Improvisation is deceptively simple. Quick workshops can provide an exciting and stimulating introduction to the work, but to reap the real benefits of improvisational training requires deeper commitment. Therefore, we wanted to create programs that would foster an ongoing relationship with the educational community. We felt we had a lot to offer teachers and students by sharing our expertise on improvisation exercises and techniques. We also felt we had a lot to learn from the educational community. We wanted to take on the challenge of exploring new applications for this work, adapting methods to suit those applications.

Through a series of discussions, we kept coming back to a core principle that guides the work at The Second City, in training center classrooms and on our professional stages: the ensemble creates the experience, moment to moment, in an ongoing process of discovery.

Our path was clear: to treat each classroom community as an ensemble. We would begin our work with the teachers, sharing wonderful tools and beginning a dialogue with the people who best understand students' needs and curriculum requirements. Through this dialogue, we would enter into a true collaboration with classroom teachers, who are in ongoing authentic relationship with the children who spend their days in their company.

From our first pilot workshop with teachers, we knew we were on the right path. The teachers responded with enthusiasm and creativity and opened our eyes to how these exercises can be used to enhance learning exploration, imagination, and the classroom community. From these initial pilot workshops, The Second City Training Center developed The Second City Improvisation for Creative Pedagogy professional development workshops for teachers. The training center also developed an artist-in-residence program that places a member of the center faculty in a classroom to work closely with the teacher in finding ways to use improvisation best suited to the needs of that particular group of students.

OVERVIEW OF THE BOOK

Building on Viola Spolin's original improvisation games and games taught at The Second City Training Center, this book explores the connections of improvisation to teaching and learning. Improvisation is profoundly effective in developing a number of skills:

Listening

Following directions

Focus

Oral communication

Team building

Empathy

Self-awareness

Self-efficacy

Self-confidence

Critical and creative problem solving

Idea generation

In addition, teachers who have used improvisation in their classroom have discovered that these exercises are infinitely adaptable.

Chapter Two draws on the Second City's commissioned research study of its educational programs; additional work by educational researchers such as Betty Jane Wagner, Jeffrey Wilhelm, and Dorothy Heathcoate; recent published connections between kinesthetic learning experiences (such as improvisation) and recent brain research; and other sources to show evidence that improvisation is a vital teaching tool that has significant impact in a traditional educational setting.

The majority of the book details a variety of specific improvisational exercises and gives examples of how they may be adapted for specific K–8 classroom learning experiences in the content areas of language arts, mathematics, science, and social studies. These examples demonstrate that improvisation can be used to teach content, build classroom community, and develop cooperative learning skills. Descriptions of improvisational games are followed with examples of lessons that classroom teachers developed at The Second City Improvisation for Creative Pedagogy professional development workshops. The lesson plans incorporate strategies and elements of curriculum differentiation, the theory of multiple intelligences, and current methodology in best practices for classroom learning. All of the lessons are linked to current expectations of Mid-continent Research for Education and Learning (MCREL) and the Ontario Ministry of Education.

The Second City is breaking new ground in creating links between improvisational techniques and classroom teaching of subject areas other than drama. This book is exceptional in that it offers educators of all content areas a variety of lessons and strategies that connect improvisational exercises to teaching through practical examples of kinesthetic and authentic learning activities.

References

Montessori, M. (1995). *The absorbent mind.* New York: Holt.

Spolin, V., quoted in *Los Angeles Times,* May 26, 1974.

Spolin, V. (1986). *Theater games for the classroom: A teacher's handbook.* Evanston, IL: Northwestern University Press.

Spolin, V. (1999). *Improvisation for the theater: A handbook of teaching and directing techniques* (3rd ed.). Evanston, IL: Northwestern University Press.

Improvisation as a Pedagogical Tool for Engaged Learning

It was more than thirteen years ago that Katie attended a National Endowment for the Humanities program for teaching Shakespeare through performance as a high school teacher. She recalls:

> At this conference I learned how to unravel the linguistic complexity of Shakespeare's text. When I returned to my high school students in a diverse urban public school, I decided to try out many of the techniques that I learned. It was 1993 and only two other colleagues used dramatic activities to teach literature. I closed my door and employed these strategies largely without sharing them with my fellow teachers. I soon realized that I needed to pitch the study guides that I regularly used with my students when teaching Shakespeare and decided to teach the plays largely through drama strategies. As my successes with these students increased, I knew that I needed to increase my repertoire of drama activities and exercises for the teaching of text.

It didn't stop there. For the past thirteen years, Katie has discovered that drama activities, particularly improvisation, were invaluable in teaching students how to work together as a team and foster an environment where risk taking is valued. She also learned that these improvisation activities are ones that foster literacy skill development in all kinds of students. It makes sense; improvisation encourages creation, analysis, and interpretation of text.

This chapter explores the connections between improvisation and engaged learning in the classroom. We first examine building community in the classroom, notions of engaged learning, and the literacy connection.

CONNECTIONS BETWEEN IMPROVISATION AND AUTHENTIC, ENGAGING TEACHING AND LEARNING EXPERIENCES

The concept of the democratic classroom is not new to the present educational paradigm (Dewey, 1938). This concept values student-directed classrooms where teachers and students work in a partnership and where self-expression is fostered through skill building. If children have a voice in the classroom, they are more

The Alphabet Game, an early-level improvisation game, engages these two students as they create their version of the letter *A*.

likely to become engaged and involved in their learning and thus more motivated to learn. Students in democratic classrooms tend to be more motivated and interested in what they are learning (Wolk, 1998). Activities such as improvisation can contribute to building this kind of learning environment. It is also the foundational Second City concept of "yes, and," that is the cornerstone for creating a democratic environment.

The concept of "yes, and" is a simple one. All ideas are valued and included in an activity. No idea is stupid or dumb. All ideas are accepted and built on. Because participants' ideas are valued and embraced, students feel affirmed and are more encouraged to take creative risks in this environment. For example, in The Second City's educational outreach programs visiting artists specifically teach the students about the "yes, and" approach and the importance of an ensemble, of working as a team. The "yes, and" approach is the improvisational concept of agreeing with what a partner in a scene or exercise offers and building on that idea or suggestion. The artists also explicitly explain the expectations they have for their adult students at The Second City. In addition to creating an environment where all ideas are accepted and all students are encouraged to participate in this democratic environment, there is also an established level of authenticity for the students. When students are exposed to these concepts of "yes, and" and authenticity, those who were previously resistant to improvisation activities are more willing to participate, and those who were already enthusiastic participants are affirmed for their work.

What is authentic learning? When we use the term *authentic* it refers to students' perception that school is relevant to them and that they are learning topics and subjects with real substance and applicability for their future. According to Newmann (1992), conditions in the area of authentic work that may engage students are work that offers extrinsic rewards, intrinsic interests, sense of ownership, connection to the real world, and fun. When students feel vested in their learning, they are more motivated.

Improvisation as a tool for teaching and learning creates opportunities for students to interact with each other and create texts that are meaningful and engaging for them. In addition, students who engage in improvisation activities in the classroom develop skills in listening, following directions, focus, oral communication, team building, empathy, self-awareness, self-confidence, critical and creative problem solving, and idea generation (see Table 2.1). All of these skills are important for students.

Table 2.1
Improvisation Activities and Skills for Learning

	SKILLS									
IMPROVISATION EXERCISES	Listening	Following Directions	Focus	Oral Communication	Team Building	Empathy	Self-Awareness	Self-Confidence	Critical and Creative Problem Solving	Idea Generation
Ad Game				x	x			x	x	x
Alphabet							x	x	x	
Beginning, Middle, End				x	x			x	x	x
Bippity, Bippity, Bop	x	x	x		x		x	x		x
Bus Trip (created by Mary Scruggs)						x	x	x		
Conducted Story	x		x	x	x			x	x	
Deck of Cards						x	x	x	x	
Dr. Know-It-All	x			x	x			x	x	
Gibberish	x		x			x	x	x	x	
Give and Take	x	x			x		x	x		
Mirror			x			x	x	x		
Object Work			x				x	x	x	
One-Word Story	x		x	x	x			x	x	
Panel of Experts				x	x			x	x	x
Parts of a Whole	x				x		x	x	x	x
Pass the Clap		x	x		x		x	x		
Slide Show				x	x			x	x	x
Space Substance			x				x	x	x	x
Space Walk			x				x	x		
String of Pearls	x		x	x	x		x	x		
Throwing Light	x		x	x				x	x	x
Who Started the Motion?		x			x		x	x		
Zip Zap Zop	x	x	x					x		

TEACHING AND LEARNING EXPERIENCES

The current model for teaching and learning promotes the idea and notion that classrooms should be interactive, where learning activities are a result of the partnership between the teacher and the students. Students have a voice in their learning and are encouraged to be active participants in the classroom. Unlike the traditional classroom, where the teacher primarily directs activities, the contemporary classroom results from the active collaboration inspired by a common quest for learning.

The contemporary classroom encourages active teaching and learning, which are powerful in student development and achievement because responsibility placed on the students is greater than in a more traditional teaching paradigm. An active approach such as improvisation is rooted in cooperation with peers as they make sense of a situation and present it to the rest of the class. Improvisation

Table 2.2
Traditional and Contemporary Classrooms

Traditional Classroom	Contemporary Classroom
The teacher is leader and demands respect.	The teacher is a guide and works side by side with the students.
Students are given class rules and are expected to follow them.	Students create class rules with the teacher's guidance. They are expected to abide by the rules.
Students can become dependent on the teacher's knowledge and passive in learning.	Students are active seekers of knowledge. The teacher acts as a guide for the students' quest for knowledge.
The teacher creates and asks most of the questions.	The students create, ask, and answer questions with the guidance of their teacher.
Students are often expected to regurgitate what they have learned on tests.	Students are active learners and demonstrate what they have learned in varied and dynamic assessments.
The classroom is usually arranged in rows, and students are expected to sit during instruction.	The classroom is a busy and active place.

is vocally, physically, and personally demanding; it requires students to make numerous kinds of presentations. Students are consistently analyzing and thinking on their feet. Improvisation is a source of deepening self-awareness in students as they find ways to express their ideas, opinions, and feelings through the physical action of improvisation. This is why improvisation belongs in a contemporary classroom.

Through the work of improvisation in teaching and learning, the development of a student's critical thinking is symbiotic to imaginative and emotional growth as students creatively solve problems through improvisation activities. Students grow intellectually and emotionally as they speculate, reason, and predict while experiencing and participating in improvisation activities. Improvisation can increase student confidence and competence in problem solving through active and engaging exercises.

Participating in the Alphabet Game, the girls
create the letter *M.*

IMPROVISATION FOR ENGAGED TEACHING AND LEARNING IN THE DIVERSE AND INCLUSIVE CLASSROOM

As our classrooms become increasingly diverse, creating opportunities where students have an active and engaged voice is crucial. Improvisation in the classroom is not a distraction from the curriculum; rather, it is a supplement and support for students to develop their skills in critical thinking, problem solving, and idea development. These skills are essential for the intellectual and emotional development of our students as citizens of a democratic society.

In addressing classroom diversity and engaged learning, we find that students with special needs are often absent from the conversation. These students also benefit from participating in improvisation activities in the classroom. Improvisation is a powerful teaching tool for students with special needs; it offers a meaningful context for collaboration and negotiation. Students with special needs are often isolated in school communities. Breaking these isolated communities and creating mixed-ability communities has been a long-term focus for many school districts. Engaging mixed-ability groups, which include students with special needs, creates a setting where students are able to transcend these barriers. When all kinds of students are able to participate in environments that encourage them to work together, they can develop trust, collaboration, and even friendship, which in turn supports them in facing social and educational challenges.

A 2005 study contracted by The Second City specifically examined the potential impact of the educational outreach program in three urban schools (McKnight, Smith, Passman, and Berlage, 2006). In the three schools that researchers visited, they observed collaboration, participation, and engagement of special needs students as the students participated in improvisation workshops conducted by visiting Second City artists. One instance included Penny, an autistic fifth grader at Lakeside Magnet School (all personal and school names are pseudonymous). When her full-time aide, Melanie, was interviewed, she remarked that Penny was more attentive and engaged when she participated in the improvisation activities; Penny interacted and successfully created polished scenes for performance with her student peers. Melanie, who had been working with her for seven months at the time of the interview, claimed that this was the most engaged and attentive that she had been all year. Melanie also commented that Penny's attentiveness often carried over to her other classes once the improvisation sessions were complete: "I am really amazed that Penny did so well with this work." Penny's regular classroom teacher, Rebecca, also confided that she was initially hesitant about

Penny's participating in the improvisation class session, because Penny's mild autism makes it difficult for her to interact and engage with a group of students. But Rebecca decided to let her try it. She shared Melanie's amazement that Penny blossomed and became more attentive in class.

The potential impact of improvisation on special needs students was also noticeable at another urban school in the study, Midtown Elementary. In a fifth to eighth grade self-contained special education class where there were a range of diagnosed disabilities among the students, it was evident that many of the students had difficulty in focusing and following directions. Coauthor Mary Scruggs was the visiting artist from Second City. She began the improvisation workshop with Pass the Clap as a means to focus the students.

Pass the Clap is often used as an introductory lesson. The participants are in a circle. One player starts the game by making eye contact with another player. Both clap their hands simultaneously. The "receiving" player then makes eye contact with another player and they synchro-clap, and so on.

As the class participated in Pass the Clap, several students had difficulty with the directions, but their understanding was facilitated through repetition of directions. For two students who had great difficulty in focusing on the activity, their classroom teacher physically moved the students' hands and repeated the directions so that they could accomplish the task. One of these students, a male seventh grader, had trouble engaging with the group as they played Pass the Clap but became better at it and noticeably relaxed and smiled. In fact, from that point on he focused on his classmates as they passed the clap and smiled as the clap moved closer to him. He was able to pass the clap many times from that point until the session was concluded. As a matter of fact, many of the students smiled at each other and established eye contact with one another. As the students played, eye contact and focus increased. The classroom teacher participating in the activity was also smiling and laughing as his students became more successful in passing the clap.

On the surface, this exercise may seem to have little educational value, but it has a great deal to do with students' education and their learning community. It is through improvisational activities such as Pass the Clap that students with special needs are able to develop their skills in collaboration, negotiation, focus, and attention, all of which are essential to learning. Smiling, laughing, collaboration, negotiation, focus, and attention are all overt indications of a community of learners.

Improvisation, a process drama, offers an environment that can strengthen student self-esteem, which is critical for special needs students. In addition, improvisation also allows a student to be courageous, powerful, thoughtful, and creative. It is through these experiences that students with special needs can see themselves as learners. They become successful among their peers. This success empowers them, strengthening their ability to act as learners. Improvisation is about recognizing one's unique perspective of the world, one's own personal voice. As students find their voice, they have the potential to express their individual thoughts and ideas and be active, contributing members of a learning community.

If students participate in creative and artistic experiences like improvisation, they become more skilled in expressing their own ideas and sharing what they know and understand within the classroom community. This development of classroom community is critical to authentic teaching and learning experiences.

THE BRAIN CONNECTION

There is substantial research in the past decade that links brain development and learning. In *Enriching the Brain* (Jensen, 2006), the author links recent brain research to effective learning strategies in the classroom. He explains that the brain is more malleable than previously thought and that if the students we teach are exposed to many stimuli, they are able to develop even more brain connections than was previously thought. Dynamic and varied teaching approaches promoting brain development are essential to cognitive development. Creative kinesthetic learning activities, characteristic of improvisation exercises, are invaluable for the classroom.

As educators, most of us are familiar with Howard Gardner's theory of multiple intelligences. Gardner (1983) asserts that there are different types of learners and that our classrooms must reflect this eclectic paradigm (see Table 2.3).

Because there are many types of learners, we need to construct classrooms that include a wide variety of learning experiences so that we can teach all students. In our current educational climate, where politicians rather than educators are making decisions about our public schools, courses such as music, art, drama, and physical education (all largely kinesthetic learning experiences) are the first subjects to be dropped in a school district, often in response to budget cuts and efforts to raise test scores. It is actually a defeating approach to teaching and learning. If anything, offering more kinesthetic experiences offering a

Table 2.3
Types of Learner According to Howard Gardner

Learner Type	Characteristics of Learner Type	Teaching Tools and Strategies	Teaching and Learning Tools Could Include:
Visual-spatial	Aware of environments, like to draw, complete puzzles, read maps.	These learners can be taught through drawings, verbal and physical imagery.	Models, graphics, charts, photographs, drawings, three-dimensional models, video, television, multimedia.
Bodily-kinesthetic	Effectively uses body.	These learners like movement, making things, and touching. They communicate best through body language.	Concrete objects, physical activities, hands-on learning, acting out, role playing.
Musical	Demonstrate sensitivity to rhythm and sound.	These learners often prefer to have music in the background while completing assignments. Can be taught through speaking rhythmically or turning lessons into lyrics.	Musical instruments, music, radio, iPod, multimedia.
Interpersonal	Interacting and understanding with others.	Learn through interaction and have many friends and demonstrate empathy. They have "street smarts." Can be taught in cooperative group activities and classroom dialogue.	Telephone, classroom discussions, e-mail, writing, computer or video conferencing.
Intrapersonal	Understand individual needs, goals, and interests. These are the most independent learners.	Often possess highly developed auditory skills and think in words. Independent study is an effective teaching strategy because they are generally intuitive and self-motivated.	Books, creative materials, privacy, and time to work on independent projects.
Linguistic	Effectively use words.	Like the intrapersonal learner, often possess highly developed auditory skills and think in words. They like reading, playing word games, and making up stories and poems.	Seeing and using words, reading books together, computers, games, books, and classroom discussion.
Logical-mathematical	These learners reason and calculate.	They are able to explore patterns and relationships because they think conceptually. These are abstract thinkers. They also need to master concepts before they can deal with details.	Experiments, puzzles, logic games, mysteries.

Y is represented by this student in the Alphabet Game, which incorporates Gardner's theory of multiple intelligences. In this game, students must represent what they know kinesthetically.

variety of learning experiences, as Jensen (2006), Gardner (1983), and others suggest, is critical to brain development and learning.

As we continue examining the types of learner and the connection to improvisation activities for teaching learning, we also need to look at gender differences. Recent brain research has led to significant understanding about how boys and girls learn. They do indeed learn differently, as is illustrated in Table 2.4.

As this table illustrates, there are distinct learning differences between boys and girls. It isn't true that boys learn better than girls or girls learn better than boys. What the research demonstrates is that they learn *differently*. Another caveat is that we should be cautious in concluding that these differences are absolute. As educators, we should think of them as general guidelines or notions. Educators know there are always exceptions; we are working with human beings having unique traits that make every one of us an individual.

How is this connected to using improvisation in the classroom? Simply, if boys need movement to learn better, it makes sense to incorporate improvisation as a teaching and learning strategy because participants are literally thinking on their feet. Students also develop language and interpersonal skills as they solve problems and work as a collaborative ensemble. In turn, girls benefit for all of the reasons that boys do, but it is interesting to note that with the stimulation of spatial thinking and kinesthetic experiences they are also developing their right brain for future activities.

This section on the brain connection began with the idea that the more and varied learning experiences students have in a classroom, the more connections the brain can develop. This is why improvisation is so valuable; it draws in all kinds of learners, both boys and girls. As they participate in improvisation exercises, they develop skill sets in both the right brain and the left and increase their ability to create a collaborative community, which is foundational to a classroom where teaching and learning is successful.

BUILDING A COMMUNITY FOR ENGAGED TEACHING AND LEARNING

About three years ago, when The Second City first embarked on improvisation exercises in the classroom, it became clear in the pilot professional development sessions with teachers that these exercises were applicable to teaching and learning in all content areas. Math teachers developed lessons that used improvisation

Table 2.4
Boys and Girls: Learning Differences

	Boys	Girls
Reasoning	Better at deductive reasoning, which often gives them an advantage on standardized tests. Generally more able to calculate in abstract. For mathematics, boys tend to learn the subject when it is taught abstractly on a chalkboard. They like to debate and explore the abstract.	Generally more comfortable and skilled in inductive reasoning. In school, it is often easier for them to give an example to explain a more general theory or concept. Girls learn mathematics better when they are taught with manipulatives.
Language development	In learning situations, boys use less language than girls and often prefer to work silently. Boys gravitate to jargon and find coded language more interesting.	Generally speaking, girls are able to produce more words than boys. In learning situations, girls use more words and oral language than boys. Jargon is not a preference for girls. Everyday language with concrete language is preferred.
Listening	Boys tend to hear less, and their hearing is often not as acute as girls'.	Girls are usually better listeners.
Focus and boredom	Boys tend to bore more easily in classrooms and need varied stimuli. Varied teaching strategies and stimuli are more effective than ignoring a student's boredom or expecting him to manage his behavior.	Girls also need varied teaching strategies and stimuli but appear to be more tolerant of classroom boredom.
Physical space	Boys like to spread out. Their spatial brains make it necessary to create space where they learn.	
Movement	The research suggests that male brains need physical movement to learn and think better. Sometimes this may appear to the teacher as fidgety behavior.	Girls usually don't fidget or demonstrate as much need for movement.
Cooperative learning	Boys attend to the task at hand rather than the social and emotional elements that are common in cooperative groups.	Cooperative learning activities are easier for girls because they are skilled in social interaction and understanding interpersonal dynamics.

Source: based on Gurian and Ballew (2003).

exercises to teach addition and subtraction. We talked to teachers about the strong literacy connection between improvisation and the skills sets that students need for reading and writing. (This is addressed more in Chapters Four and Five.) In addition, teachers also reported that their students worked together better as a community in the classroom.

In the 2005 study mentioned earlier, researchers found important links to participation in improvisation exercises and classroom community (McKnight, Smith, Passman, and Berlage, 2006). The researchers observed during the residencies (and it was confirmed by teachers' reports) that The Second City educational program served to build community and collaboration among the students in the classrooms where the trainers worked. In the three schools in the study and in each participating classroom, the Second City trainers diligently worked to develop a positive atmosphere for risk taking as they taught improvisation techniques, and they connected the improvisation work to the kind of human interaction that young people might encounter outside of school life. The trainers we observed taught specifically about the "yes, and" approach (Spolin, 1986) and the importance of ensemble (as explained in Chapter One). The Second City trainers and artists in residence were also explicit with the students about the types of behavior and attitude expected of adults when they come to The Second City for training or are part of Second City performances. Framing the expectations in this way established a level of authenticity (Newmann, 1992) that facilitated bringing those students who were initially resistant to the processes into the work and affirmed the work of those who had been enthusiastic from the start.

For example, Mary recalls that while observing instances when the stories the students groups were developing took a violent turn, they seemed to be pushing to find the boundaries of acceptable language and actions. In each case, Mary pointed out that "with adult actors at Second City, we usually don't improvise violence; we usually don't improvise weapons" and went on to explain what a negative impact violence has on the comedic effect of a story and on the dynamics of a group of actors. Her positive emphasis on moving the work forward, rather than on the students' negative behavior, had a positive impact on each of the groups, and the students shifted from finding ways to push the limits to finding ways to contribute. Not all groups in all schools made equal positive growth, but in all groups observed cooperative behavior did increase over the course of the time in which the trainers were present, and students supported one another's efforts by applauding, offering positive feedback, and building on one another's ideas.

For some groups of students, the attitude of acceptance that these lessons engendered seemed to translate into other areas of classroom life. According to an eighth grade teacher from the 2005 study, her students carried the ideas into their classroom work. While students were working on a project unrelated to the Second City workshops, she overheard one student say to another, "Yes, and, remember? Let's take your idea and add to it . . ." (McKnight, Smith, Passman, and Berlage, 2006).

The current paradigm for education advocates for dynamic classrooms where students are actively participating in a variety of learning experiences. Recent research in education and brain development supports this model for teaching and learning. Improvisation exercises engage students in varied learning experiences where they develop their skills and competency in all content areas. The next three chapters illustrate and develop the improvisation, teaching, and learning connection.

References

Dewey, J. (1938). *Experience and education.* New York: Macmillan.

Gardner, H. (1983). *Frames of mind: The theory of multiple intelligences.* New York: Basic Books.

Gurian, M., & Ballew, A. (2003). *The boys and girls learn differently action guide for teachers.* San Francisco: Jossey-Bass.

Jensen, E. (2006). *Enriching the brain: How to maximize every learner's potential.* San Francisco: Jossey-Bass.

McKnight, K., Smith, K., Passman, R., & Berlage, B. (2006). Improvisation, creative pedagogy, and learning in the urban classroom: The Second City Educational Program. Unpublished study.

Newmann, F. M. (1992). *Student engagement and achievement in American secondary schools.* New York: Teachers College Press.

Spolin, V. (1986). *Theater games for the classroom.* Evanston, IL: Northwestern University Press.

Wolk, S. (1998). *A democratic classroom.* Portsmouth, NH: Heinemann.

Literacy Learning
and Improvisation

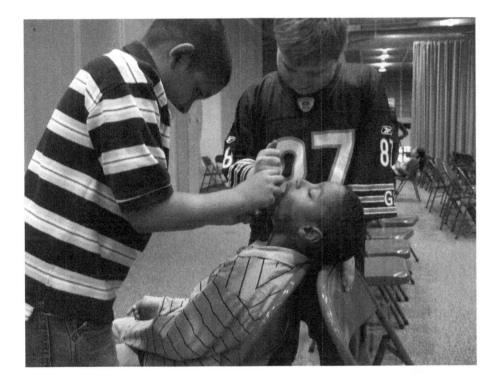

Three fourth grade boys intently use object work to
recreate a scene at the dentist's office. Notice the focus
and concentration of these students.

More than three years ago, at a meeting at The Second City we
discussed the connections between improvisational exercises
and literacy development. Mary teaches sketch writing at the Second

City, and the improvisation exercises and games are the springboard for scripts. As a teacher of adolescents and future teachers, Katie saw real connections between improvisational exercises and literacy. Creating "text" through improvisation is quite similar to the creation and comprehension of text in an education setting.

When we teach literacy in schools, we teach our students about the meaning of text and how we can create it. We also teach students skills in decoding and comprehending text. Prediction, sequencing, vocabulary building, inferencing, and reflection are skills that are used in improvisation exercises as well as lessons that encourage and develop students' literacy skills.

POTENTIAL IMPACT ON LITERACY SKILL DEVELOPMENT

There are significant links between improvisation and development of students' skill sets in literacy. Reading, writing, and other literacies are unique and powerful ways of knowing about self, others, and the world. Improvisation is not dissimilar, creating opportunities for students to develop these literacy skill sets.

When we think of literacy, we often think it is primarily about the written word. Literacy is much greater; it is anything that creates story (Probst, 2004; Rosenblatt, 1978, 1995; Wilhelm, 2007). Through improvisation, any student can create meaning. As we witnessed in many schools that partnered with The Second City, students clearly develop literacy skills through improvisation activities. Methods such as improvisation facilitate a student's ability to unlock textual meaning. Teachers and researchers often comment that students who participate in dramatic activities such as improvisation confide that they are able to understand text when they act it out because they figure it out (McKnight, 2000; Wilhelm, 2007).

IMPROVISATION AND READING LINKS

Before we begin a comparison of the links between reading instruction and improvisation, we want to review what we know about teaching reading and how it is situated with other literacies such as writing and oral language. Currently, balanced literacy is a common framework in today's schools. In short, a balanced

Table 3.1
Comparing Reading Instruction in a Balanced Literacy Program to Improvisation Exercises in the Classroom

Improvisation Exercises	Reading Instruction in Balanced Literacy Program
Grouping is spontaneous and changes with almost every exercise.	Student grouping is dynamic and flexible. The composition of the groups regularly changes.
Skill development is embedded within the literacy activity. Participants learn by doing (Spolin, 1986).	Skills development and practice is embedded within the literacy activity.
Focus is on the participant and contribution to the ensemble.	Focus is on the student, not the exercise.
Teacher actively participates and is a member of the ensemble.	Teacher actively participates and interacts with the students.
Teacher and students actively participate and interact in the improvisation exercise.	Teacher and students actively interact with the text.
"Sidecoaching" is designed to aid the participants in problem solving as the students participate in the improvisation activity.	Questions are created to develop higher-order thinking skills and to actively solve problems.
The participants are focused on presenting dramatic representations that communicate clearly to the audience. In other words, the meaning that the participants create must be understood by the audience.	The students are focusing in understanding meaning from the text.
Students create and respond in the exercise with personal, authentic, and meaningful representations and interpretations.	Students respond to the story through personal and authentic exercises.
Students create independently as members of a creative ensemble.	Students read independently.
Assessment is ongoing and continuous through peer and teacher feedback.	Assessment is ongoing and continuous through peer and teacher feedback.

framework is an approach to teaching readers and writers effectively. It is solidly grounded in the idea that all students can read and write well. In a balanced literacy classroom, the students are engaging in a collaborative environment through a variety of literacy activities that could include read-alouds, guided reading, literature circles, and vocabulary (Fountas and Pinnell, 2001). The foundational ideas for balanced literacy instruction are not all that different from the foundational concepts in the Second City improvisation games, where all participants can creatively contribute to craft a successful dramatic experience. In both balanced literacy experiences and improvisation games, the goal is to successfully create a shared authentic experience. In addition, balanced literacy allows students to work at their own level through differentiated instruction. Again, this is not dissimilar to improvisation in the Second City philosophy, which we learn from doing the improvisation games. Once they participate in the improvisation games, students grow clearer about how improvisation works. Again, this is akin to the balanced literacy approach. Students develop their literacy skill sets when they are the ones who are actively participating in literacy activities in the classroom.

Engaging students in reading so that they can evoke and exert control over the ideas, sensations, characters, and meanings that are experienced can be developed through improvisation. Louise Rosenblatt, a foundational theorist for reader response theory, discussed the connections between reading and creative activity: "The benefits of literature can emerge only from creative activity on the part of the reader himself" (1978, p. 276). As with improvisation, where the actor must create meaning through exploration, reading demands involvement and participation in the text. The connections between reader response and improvisation are a critical component in the examining reading and other literacies such as writing and improvisation.

Rosenblatt (1978) describes the connection between reading (specifically literature) and drama: "We accept the fact that the actor infuses his own voice, his own body, his own gestures—in short, his own interpretation—into the words of the text. Is he not carrying to its ultimate manifestations what each of us as readers of text must do?" (p. 13).

Are we, as readers, dissimilar to actors? Like actors, if we are engaged readers, then we are allowing ourselves to participate in the imaginary text worlds. Reading literature, according to Rosenblatt (1995), is the reader's participation in a "transaction" with text that produces meaning.

These students participate in the Mirror game, which develops focus and concentration.

For less engaged readers, who are often the students having The most difficulty reading challenging text, creative dramatics can aid understanding of the text. The act of reading is described as the creation of "secondary worlds" (Britton, 1970) and the involvement and enactment of drama within these text worlds. If readers are placed into this secondary world through creative dramatics such as improvisation, then they are experiencing and reacting to the text from within. This kind of participant stance that the reader takes allows him or her to participate in this text world rather than being a spectator. As we took field notes during this study, we observed these secondary worlds on several occasions. For example, here is an experience from fifth grade students at an elementary school in Chicago who created a secondary text world through improvisation.

Coauthor Mary was the artist in residence from The Second City, working with a group of energetic and kinetic boys. In many of the improvisation activities that we observed, this group of boys literally bounced off the walls. During one improvisation activity, Mary stopped the boys and asked, "Hey, let me see that again." The boys recreated a scene where they hunted an animal; they revealed that the scene came from the Native American stories they had been reading. The students told Mary about some of the story elements and that they were recreating text they had already read. Mary stopped and thought about all that they revealed. She decided to sit them in a circle, and once she had their complete focus, she asked, "What is your scene about? What's going on here?" The boys explained quite simply that they were hunters and were chasing an animal. "Where's the animal?" Mary asked. The boys looked at each other and quickly chose Darnell, who smiled and accepted the role. The boys decided that the animal in the scene was a fox. Mary prompted the students to do the scene again. Before the students performed, Mary pulled Darnell aside and asked him if he could make us believe that he was a fox. Darnell smiled and declared, "No problem." Using his legs and arms, he created an amazing four-legged physical representation of the fox, who then became known as Chico. Darnell's classmates cheered and offered many compliments.

Over several sessions, the boys eventually developed a complete story about a magical fox that was hunted by a group of Native Americans (this contributed to their fifth grade thematic unit on Native Americans). They were influenced by the stories they read and researched about Native Americans. Their original simple skit evolved into a fable about Chico the fox. The Native American hunters sought to kill or capture Chico, but the fox escaped and transformed into a double-sized being. In response to Mary's prompting, the boys decided that the moral of the story was "Never be jealous of an animal's power."

The students rehearsed several times over the course of two weeks, and eventually they videotaped the fable. Mary offered some last-minute instructions to the actors, and the taping commenced. Once the taping was complete, the student actors were eager to view the performance. They were enraptured in watching the video. Mary and the fifth grade teachers had never seen the students so engaged.

In working with these fifth grade boys, Mary is reminded of the birthday cake analogy: you've got to have a mess before the cake is ready. Mary offered, "They [the fifth grade boys] want the cake on the second day, and all they can see is the mess." They clearly learned that the birthday cake takes more than two days to create; the boys learned this lesson and decided they wanted to make some improvements and tape their fable again.

In this case, the students developed an original text and secondary world that allowed them ample opportunity to practice and develop a number of literacy skills: speaking, listening, comprehension, visualization, representation, sequencing, synthesis of information, elaboration, and understanding of literary genre and elements of story.

Thinking of teaching methods and strategies that catapult a student into the text is a paramount pedagogical concern for schools that want to develop students' literacy skill sets. Improvisation is one pedagogical strategy that can develop a student's ability to "see text" (Table 3.2). When students see text, they can develop their ability to decipher and comprehend text as well as create expressive text through writing.

In the case of drama, these activities help reluctant readers enter texts and respond. They are able to open their notions of reading as well as strategies for reading. It reinforces the necessity of drawing on the reader's prior experience to create meaning. Students are encouraged to explore and create new meaning as they enter text worlds (Wilhelm, 2007).

IMPROVISATION AND WRITING LINKS

There are strong links between writing and improvisation exercises. As with reading, the current model for teaching writing is built on a framework that encourages collaboration and creating text that is authentic and personally meaningful.

Table 3.2
Literacy Skill Sets Developed Through Improvisation

Skills	Reading	Writing	Speaking	Listening
Vocabulary development	X	X	X	X
Sequencing	X	X	X	
Prediction	X	X	X	X
Representation of nonlinguistic text			X	
Adding details to textual representations		X	X	
Focus	X	X	X	X
Concentration	X	X	X	X
Interpretation	X	X	X	X
Synthesis of information	X	X	X	X
Developing an understanding and appreciation of literary genres	X	X		
Idea and topic generation		X	X	
Active exploration of student author's voice		X	X	
Appropriate use of oral language			X	
Analysis of context in both linguistic and nonlinguistic text	X	X	X	X

At first glance, using improvisation to help students who have low literacy skills is especially attractive, because so many of these students find writing a frustrating, even painful experience. Teachers, armed with rubrics outlining what makes good writing, feel their own frustration in trying to help these students. The directive to "add more detail" is mystifying to a student with limited vocabulary. The suggestion to "support the main idea with specific examples" is daunting to a student who can't articulate the main idea. For any student with poor grammar and spelling skills or dysgraphia, the very act of putting words down on paper is demoralizing or even humiliating.

Obviously, improvisation is a wonderful way to reach these students, to let them experience firsthand the joy of fluent communication. Using improvisation, students can experience the thrill of exploring an idea, creating a character, experiencing an environment, using an object, or telling a story—usually on a far more complex and sophisticated level than they can on paper.

This experience benefits students at every level of proficiency because it separates thinking and creating from the physical act of writing. When students do sit down to put their improvisational experiences into written form, their story or essay or description is already more or less finished; they just need to document it. Freed from the task of trying to think of something to write, students are focused on recording what was a thrilling experience for the purpose of not only communicating it but making it permanent.

Improvisation specifically develops necessary writing skills:

• *Prewriting.* By definition, prewriting is the first stage of the writing process, where students generate topics and ideas for writing. Student participation in improvisation exercises such as String of Pearls; Beginning, Middle, End; and One-Word Story involves writing topics.

• *Personal narrative.* Because all writing begins with the personal narrative (Murray, 2003), improvisation also draws on the participants' personal experiences. Drawing out personal stories can lead to creating written text.

• *Details.* In our work with young writers, it is most often cited in feedback and suggestions for revision that more details need to be added to a particular draft of writing. Improvisation games that help student writers develop a sense of necessary details for written text include Parts of a Whole, String of Pearls, Object Work, One-Word Story, and Conducted Story.

• *Vocabulary.* Related to developing a sense for details in writing is the need to expand personal vocabulary. Improvisation games such as Parts of a Whole, One-Word Story, and Object Work support development of vocabulary.

• *Story elements: plot, character, and conflict.* These essential story elements are integral to both writing and improvisation exercises. Nearly every improvisation exercise aids student writers in developing these story elements, but there are several that are particularly useful: One-Word Story; Beginning, Middle, End; Conducted Story; Slide Show; and String of Pearls. As we began this chapter, we discussed the definition of literacy. When we think of literacy today, it extends beyond reading and writing. It is a process of coming to know and understand the world that surrounds us. In this chapter, we have already explored the connection of improvisation to reading and writing, but there is a synergetic relationship to oral language as well, specifically speaking and listening.

IMPROVISATION LINKS TO SPEAKING AND LISTENING

Of all of the major literacy skills (reading, writing, speaking, and listening), it is the last two oral language skills that are probably the most neglected in our classrooms. Learning how to be a good listener and speaker is a skill that needs

Middle school students practice their skills in creating text as they participate in improvisation.

to be developed with curriculum designed for teaching students how to effectively use oral language. Nearly every improvisation exercise teaches some aspect of listening and speaking.

Before we look more closely at the connection between listening and speaking and improvisation, we need to delve more into the characteristics and importance of teaching oral language. In classrooms, teachers often explain, lecture, question, or reprimand while students are required to listen and reply, or they whisper to their friends. Oral language continues in the hallways, labs, workshops, and playground. Our students' school day is saturated in oral language. Yet of all the literacy experiences (reading, writing, speaking, and listening), oral language is probably the most neglected and is taught in isolated fragmented units. In teaching speaking and listening, we have to remember a few important points:

- Students' levels of competency in oral language differ.
- Not all students enter school with equal levels of verbal interaction at home.
- Oral language skills are developmental. Students will not progress at the same rate.
- Just as in writing instruction, students need authentic, varied, and purposeful communication.
- Teachers need to create contexts where oral communication is valued and authentic.
- Oral language skills should be integrated into the literacy curriculum alongside reading and writing.
- Speaking and listening are not just oral. Students need to learn about eye contact, body language, and gesture to learn how they too contribute to speaking and listening.

As was already explained in the previous chapters, the improvisation games and exercises enhance and support academic, personal, and social skills. Specifically, among these areas improvisation improves all of the language and literacy skills, analytic thinking, creative problem solving, and focus and concentration. In fact, "improvisational drama, perhaps more than other oral language activities, ties directly into both literacy and nonverbal knowing"

(Wagner, 1990, p. 196). Furthermore, "Role playing and improvisation expand the boundaries of experience for students so that they develop a more complete understanding of themselves and of the literature that they are learning" (Bushman and Bushman, 1993, p. 35). Clearly, the developmental relationship between the interrelated literacies of reading, writing, speaking, and listening can be supported and nurtured with improvisational drama activities. Bushman and Bushman also assert that oral language activities such as improvisation help students "get inside the characters and play out their emotions, making choices and decisions based on the readers' understanding of those characters" (p. 35). Improvisation exercises demand that the participants employ analytic and problem-solving skills that are needed for successful role playing. Through the vicarious experiences of improvisation, students can reexamine their decisions and interpretations about text. As improvisers, students must use their speaking and listening skills to be inventor, actor, and interpreter.

We must also note that improvisation can be an important experience for limited English proficient students. You may recall from the introductory chapter that these improvisation exercises were developed partly out of the need for Viola Spolin to be able to better communicate with the mostly immigrant children that she taught at Hull House in Chicago. Second language acquisition is dependent on lively, interesting, and authentic oral language experiences. Improvisation offers this kind of experience (Moffet and Wagner, 1992).

SOME CONCLUDING THOUGHTS

Improvisation in the classroom creates pressure for students to develop their literacy skills so they are better able to send and receive messages that communicate their ideas and opinions in the classroom. We believe that the educational value of informal drama activities such as improvisation is grossly underestimated. These activities do not take away from literacy activities such as reading and writing; rather, they are critical to the development of these skills.

At a time when the current classroom model for teaching literacy calls for instruction that embraces student developmental and learning differences through a balanced literacy program, this instructional approach is a contributing factor in creation of an environment where literacy is privileged. Improvisation can have a significant impact on furthering our literacy goals for students.

References

Britton, J. (1970). *Language and learning.* New York: Penguin.

Bushman, J., & Bushman, K. P. (1993). *Using young adult literature in the English classroom.* Upper Saddle River, NJ: Merrill/Prentice Hall.

Fountas, I., & Pinnell, G. S. (2001). *Guiding readers and writers: Teaching comprehension, genre, and content literacy.* Portsmouth, NH: Heinemann.

McKnight, K. S. (2000). *Firing the canon: An examination of teaching methods for engaging high school students in canonical literature.* Unpublished dissertation, University of Illinois, Chicago.

McKnight, K., Smith, K., Passman, R., & Berlage, B. (2006). Improvisation, creative pedagogy, and learning in the urban classroom: The Second City Educational Program. Unpublished study.

Moffet, J., & Wagner, B. J. (1992). *Student-centered language arts, K–12* (4th ed.). Portsmouth, NH: Boynton/Cook, Heinemann.

Murray, D. (2003). *A writer teaches writing* (rev. ed.). Portsmouth, NH: Heinemann.

Probst, R. (2004). *Response and analysis* (2nd ed.). Portsmouth, NH: Heinemann.

Rosenblatt, L. (1978). *The reader, the text, the poem: The transactional theory of the literary work.* Carbondale: Southern Illinois University Press.

Rosenblatt, L. (1995). *Literature as exploration* (5th ed.). New York: Modern Language Association.

Wagner, B. J. (1990). Dramatic improvisation in the classroom. In S. Hynds and D. Rubin (Eds.), *Perspectives on talk and learning,* pp. 195–212. Urbana: National Council of Teachers of English.

Wilhelm, J. (2007). *You gotta be the book* (2nd ed.). New York: Teachers College Press.

Explanation of Improvisation Exercises

We have already explored the connections between improvisation exercises and classroom teaching and learning. This chapter identifies and details a variety of specific improvisational exercises that can be adapted for specific K–8 classroom learning experiences in the content areas of language arts, mathematics, science, and social studies. These exercises can be used to teach content, build classroom community, and develop cooperative learning skills. Please note that these exercises can be used for a variety of classroom learning experiences.

GETTING STARTED

It is the nature of improvisation exercises that they make more sense when students do them rather than when teachers explain them. Therefore, instructions should be simple and clear; the goal is to engage students in the exercise as soon as possible. To a large extent, the exercise itself teaches everyone in the classroom—students and teachers—how the exercise works.

The challenge, of course, is trusting this process. For many teachers the temptation to jump in and tell the students how to do it the right way is often overwhelming. It's very important for adults in the classroom to resist this

Many students develop focus and concentration through improvisation exercises.

temptation; doing so erodes the very foundation we're trying to build by using improvisation in the first place. Many of us charged with the responsibility of teaching children believe our proficiency is judged by our students' success, and the most talented, skilled teachers get their students to reach a successful outcome the fastest. But to really embrace improvisation in the classroom is to give ourselves permission to engage in a process of discovery with our students.

TIME FOR IMPROVISATION

Improvisation activities, if they are taught in school at all, are traditionally part of a drama curriculum. Typically, this confines the activities to a special time and place. This means a walk away from the classroom to a special setting—a lunchroom, an auditorium, or any large open space. If a school is lucky enough to have the resources for drama activities, they are often just one component of an arts enrichment program, which means that drama shares time on the schedule with visual arts and music. This sends a not-so-subtle message to the students that there's a separate time and place for fun and games and that arts activities aren't part of the real, serious work that takes place in the classroom.

Improvisation for creative pedagogy calls for another approach. Improvisation games can be incorporated into any lesson, along with creating collages, writing paragraphs, reading content-specific texts, giving oral presentations, making dioramas, breaking into small groups for discussion—any of the dozens of activities creative teachers use to help their students deeply understand curriculum content.

Improvisation doesn't need special materials. There is nothing to set up or clean up when it's over. Once learned, many of the exercises take just a few minutes to play. Extended play has benefits, but it isn't necessary to set aside a whole class period to improvise; ten minutes or so is enough time to incorporate these activities into the classroom.

Many teachers use these activities as part of a larger strategy for classroom management. A quick round of improvisation can be used as a reward, as part of a transition from one subject to the next, or simply as a way to refocus and reactivate students who have been sitting too long.

Students respond as a focused ensemble.

CLASSROOM MANAGEMENT

It may seem like a bit of a paradox that the best way to create an environment for free exploration is to establish clear boundaries. Many of these boundaries are already part of the culture of most classrooms, but here is a list of the basics:

• *Designate a clearly defined playing area.* You can use the front of the classroom, with or without rows of desks pushed back. If you have a large classroom with an area already cleared for reading stories, circle activities, or learning centers, you can use that area. Be clear with students about the boundaries of the playing area.

• *Getting into and out of the exercise.* Clear expectations and dependable routines help your students transition into and out of improvisation activities without losing focus.

• *Divide students into teams.* One or two teams at a time will play the game while the others watch. Students learn by doing the exercises, and they also learn by watching each other do the exercises. Sometimes students are less attentive when they are in the audience. Encourage students to stay fully engaged by telling them you are only going to give the directions once; each group should watch those in performance to review and understand how the exercise is played. Remind students that the less time you spend giving directions, the more time they spend playing. Certain exercises, such as Mirror, can be played by the whole class at once, working in pairs.

• *The back line.* Some exercises call for a "back line" formation: the players line up at the back of the stage and step forward to participate. In playing all exercises, it is useful to ask teams of players to move from their seats into a back line, not just move into the playing area. The back line is ready to go when all students are in position, focused and alert.

• *The amount of space needed varies with the exercise, and even this can be adapted.* Most of the exercises don't need much more space than a typical classroom has at the front. The majority of the exercises can be adapted so that students perform them in their seats. A few of the exercises function best with a fairly large playing area so that twelve or more students can play at once. For these exercises, rearranging desks is the best option if you can't move to a large, open space.

• *Redirecting inappropriate behavior and subject matter.* No matter what their age, beginning improvisers are infamous for testing boundaries. Listening to the chatter in the teachers lounge at The Second City Training Center, you often can't tell if teachers are comparing notes on nine-year-olds or twenty-nine-year-olds. Teachers often feel hypocritical when they encourage their students to create, explore, and express and then are horrified by what is being created, explored, and expressed. It is a normal part of creative development to test boundaries, just as it is a normal part of human development. Martin DeMaat, the late artistic director of The Second City Training Center, would often refer (affectionately) to students as being "in the throes of artistic adolescence."

Students are expected to test boundaries; the teacher is expected to define and maintain them. Remember that students who cross boundaries are creating problems not just for the teacher; they are creating an unsafe environment for the rest of the class. Here is a list of typical situations and suggested ways of handling them.

• *Inappropriate touching.* Most exercises don't necessitate any physical contact at all; some are harder to play without some contact. In either situation, the best way to handle inappropriate touching is how a coach handles it in sports: bench the player until she cools off and then send her back into the game. Inappropriate touching often arises out of the excitement of the exercise and usually takes the form of pushing and bumping into other players. No need to admonish or lecture. Simply state the boundaries to the player, state how that boundary was crossed, and give her a time out. Most important, give her another chance to play the game.

• *Inappropriate language.* Most classrooms have well-established rules about acceptable language for the classroom; there is no need to change those rules for improvisation activities, even when students are playing characters other than themselves. Again, the time-out technique is useful for correcting this behavior.

• *Improvising violence and sexually explicit situations.* Many beginning improvisers do this; adult students do it, and they do it regardless of educational level, cultural background, how much television they do or do not watch, and how many books they do or do not read. When children improvise violence or sexually explicit situations, it can be very disturbing to adults. It is helpful to stay objective about the situation and keep everyone focused on the work. In addition to pointing out that some subjects are simply inappropriate in a classroom community, remind students to find other ways to explore conflict and relationships onstage.

SIDECOACHING AND REFLECTION

Most teachers are familiar with the technique of sidecoaching, although they may not refer to it by that name. Sidecoaching is simply making suggestions to students while they are engaged in the exercise. At its best, sidecoaching is short and specific and keeps teachers and students focused on the work and solving problems. At its worst, sidecoaching is narrative and intrusive. Effective sidecoaching is objective and nonjudgmental, and it avoids the language of success and failure. Of course, good sidecoaching is as positive as possible.

Better Sidecoaching: Instead of . . .	Try . . .
"Don't say no."	"Say, 'Yes, and. . . .' "
"That's a funny face!"	"Show how you're feeling."
"Don't stand so close to each other."	"Use the whole playing area!"
"Stop mumbling!"	"Share your voice with us."
"Don't turn your back."	"Stage picture!"
"Be more specific with that basket."	"How heavy is the basket?"
"Don't be so silly."	"Work together."
"Great! Great!"	"Keep exploring that!"

Spolin had this to say: "Sidecoaching alters the traditional relationship between teacher and student, creating a moving relation. It allows the teacher an opportunity to step into the space and learn with the players" (Spolin, 1986, p. 28).

It is helpful to discuss sidecoaching with students when you first begin introducing improvisation exercises in the classroom, so they know what to expect. Tell them that even though you will be speaking to them, they don't need to stop the exercise or look at you. Let them know they can show you that they are listening by adjusting or changing what they are doing in the activities according to your suggestions. In the beginning, as students get used to the technique of sidecoaching, it can be helpful to call for a freeze in the action, sidecoach, and then continue.

It is useful to invite students to reflect on their experiences with improvisation exercises, either through journaling or discussion. Questions that focus on process and the learner's experience of the work are most appropriate. Especially in the beginning, questions that invite the audience to critique the relative entertainment value of the exercises are less appropriate. For example, move from "Did you think that was funny?" to "What was the best part?" or "What was boring?"

Here are some sample reflection questions:

"Did you react to what the other players said or did?"

"Did you try to direct the other players?"

"Were you surprised by what happened?"

"How was this exercise different from creating something by yourself?"

"Did you try to plan or predict what would happen?"

"What would make this exercise work even better the next time?"

"How did it feel to give and take (or mirror your partner, or create a story together, and so on)? Why?"

"When you were watching, what did you notice that you might like to try to the next time you do the exercise?"

IMPROVISATION GAMES
AD GAME

Overview: In small groups, students act as a creative team working to advertise a new product. Skills are developed in oral communication, team building, self-confidence, critical and creative problem solving, and idea generation.

Instructions

- Divide students into groups of five to eight.
- Send one group to the playing area to form a back line.
- Ask the audience for a suggestion for "a new product—something no one has seen before!"
- Tell the players that they are now an advertising team, and it is their job to describe this product and inform the public about how great it is.
- Players build on everything that is said by beginning each sentence with "Yes! And...."

Sidecoaching

- "Say 'Yes! And....'"
- "Take that idea and tell us more!"

Example   The audience suggestion is "a money-generating wallet."

Marco: This great new product is a wallet—and it's never empty.

William: Yes, and it's full of hundred-dollar bills.

Anna: They grow on their own!

Teacher: Say "Yes, and...."

Anna: Yes! And they grow on their own!

Ranjit: Yes, and all you have to do is water the wallet to make them grow.

Ellie: Yes, and the wallet is waterproof.

Gabriel: Yes, and the wallet can grow vegetables.

Marco: Uh—

Teacher: Take that idea and build on it!

Marco: Uh—

Teacher: The wallet can grow vegetables, yes! And. . . .

Marco: —it can grow tomatoes!

Anna: Yes! And the wallet has a kitchen in it so you can cook the tomatoes.

Tips

- Have students brainstorm a list of several new products before you start. Then you won't have to pause in between exercises waiting for new suggestions; you can read them from your list.

- Use sidecoaching to keep the energy up and the ideas flowing, not to suggest your own ideas.

- All ideas are accepted and built on.

- "Yes, and . . . " is at the core of all improvisation and is a powerful tool for creating a environment that is conducive to cooperative learning.

ALPHABET

Overview: Students create letters of the alphabet using their bodies.

Skills are developed in self-awareness, self-confidence, and critical and creative problem solving.

Students physicalize letters of the alphabet. Notice that the teacher demonstrates and participates in the activity.

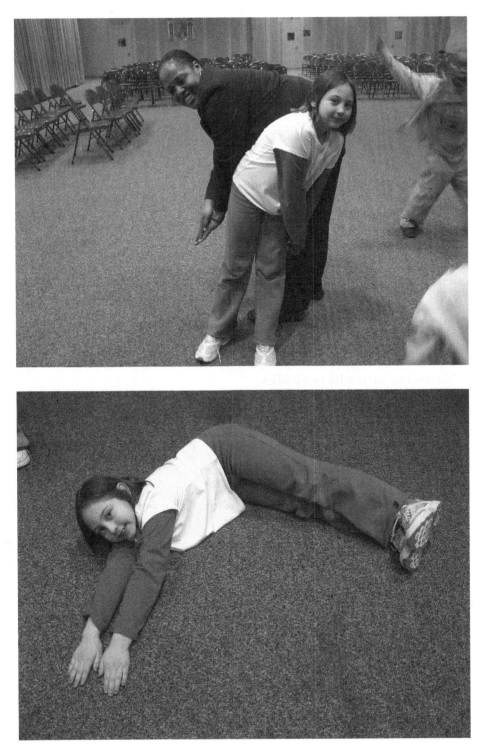

Instructions

- Space permitting, invite all students into the playing area. If there isn't enough space, divide the class into the largest groups possible to work in your playing area.
- Tell students they will work in their own personal space; they should create enough space between each other so they can work without bumping into each other.
- Tell students to use their whole body to create each letter of the alphabet as you call it out.
- If necessary, repeat until all students have had a chance to create letters with their body.
- Now, pair students and tell them to work with their partner to create each letter of the alphabet as you call it out.

Sidecoaching

"Use your whole body."

"Don't direct each other; just create."

"Work together."

"Create one letter with two bodies."

Tips

- In each round, instruct students to create either uppercase or lowercase letters, rather than doing both.
- Accept the various ways students create letters—they might lie flat on the ground or present letters backwards—as long as they use their whole body to make the letters.
- Keep the exercise moving quickly; don't take time out to correct, adjust, or comment.

Variations

- Call out sounds, and have students create the letters that make those sounds.
- Students can work in larger groups to create words.

Word families: two students can embody a common consonant blend (such as "bl") and stand in place while other groups of students join them to create words called out by the teacher, such as *bland, blend,* and *blow.*

BEGINNING, MIDDLE, END

Overview: Students create three-line stories.

Skills are developed in oral communication, team building, self-confidence, critical and creative problem solving, and idea generation.

Instructions

- Divide students into small groups of six to twelve students.
- Send one group to the playing area to form a back line.
- Working from the audience's left, bring the first student to the front. This student is the beginning.
- Bring the next student to stand next to the beginning. This student is the middle.
- Now, the third student gets into place for the end.
- Tell the students that each one of them will supply one line for the story.
- After they have told their story, just the beginning student moves to the end of the line, audience right.
- Now the middle student is the beginning, the end student is the middle, and there is a new student for the end.
- Continue until all players have cycled through the line two or three times.

Sidecoaching

"Tell us what happens next!"

"Listen to each other."

"Now a new beginning!"

"How does it end?"

"Beginning goes to the end of the line, and here comes a new end!"

Example

Blaine: Once upon a time there was a prince who believed all the girls were in love with him because he was so handsome.

Jessica: And he was right, but there was actually one princess who didn't think he was handsome at all.

Mark: The prince got mad.

Teacher: New story—beginning, get back in line—let's get a new end—go!

Jessica: Once upon a time, there was a cat who liked to sleep in the window.

Mark: The cat, uh . . . he sleeps in the window of the house.

Teacher: And what happened?

Mark: Uh—

Teacher: The cat sleeps in the window and—

Mark: Uh . . . he sleeps, and then he woke up.

Boaz: Some dogs were fighting.

Teaching: New story! Go!

Mark: One time this guy named Marko the Magnificent built a spaceship.

Boaz: The dogs, they were always fighting because everyone said they were bad.

Samara: Spaceships are OK.

Teacher: New story—build on the ideas. Listen!

Boaz: There was this musician who had a magic piano.

Teacher: Tell us what happens.

Samara: The magic piano granted wishes.

Teacher: Tell us what happens.

Ibro: The wishes didn't always turn out so good.

Tips

- Keep the exercise moving, even if the stories don't make sense.

- Use the reflection time between rounds to ask students what makes a good beginning, middle, or end.

- Reinforce what students discover on their own. Typically, early discoveries include finding that:

  - They don't need to start every story with "Once upon a time. . . ."

  - It's confusing when someone forgets to build on the established idea.

  - It's satisfying when students create cause-and-effect relationships among the beginning, middle, and end.

  - It's easier when students simply listen to each other and say what comes to mind, rather than trying to plan something in advance.

- If a student is stuck, it's helpful for the teacher to repeat what was just said; but it's important to refrain from supplying story ideas.

- This exercise is excellent for brainstorming ideas for writing assignments.

Variations include Situation, Problem, Solution; Action, Reaction, Consequence; Hypothesis, Experiment, Conclusion; Mystery, Clues, Solution.

BIPPITY, BIPPITY, BOP

Overview: This fast-paced game is played in a circle and requires players to listen and work together to avoid ending up in the center of the circle.

Skills are developed in listening, following directions, focus, team building, self-awareness, self-confidence, and idea generation.

Instructions for the Basic Game

- Up to fifteen players form a circle.
- One student goes to the center.
- The center player approaches any player in the circle, makes eye contact, and says, "Bippity, bippity, bop."
- This chosen player must say "Bop" before the center player says it.
- To trip up the circle players even further, the center player can skip "Bippity, bippity" and just say "Bop."
- If the center play beats the circle player and says "Bop" first, they trade places.

Instructions for the Advanced Game

- Once students can play the basic game, they can add pictures, which are the fun part. Each mini-tableau uses three students.
- "Elephant"—student in the center creates the trunk with her arms; students on each side create big ears with their arms.
- "Hula"—student in the center does a hula dance; students on each side wave their arms like palm trees.
- "Truck"—student in the center steers and honks the horn; students on each side show the circular motion of the wheels with their arms.
- "Movie star"—student in the center poses and blows kisses; students on either side are the camera-snapping paparazzi.
- "Airplane"—student in the center creates goggles over his eyes with his hands; students on each side create the wings with their arms.

Once students practice creating these pictures, they can incorporate them into the game. The player in the center can now use three techniques to trip up a circle player: "Bippity, bippity, bop," or "Bop" alone, or calling for a picture. To call for a picture, she points at a player, shouts the name of the picture, and then immediately starts counting, "One, two, three, four, five." The student she has pointed at, along with the students on either side, have that amount of time to create the picture.

If more two or more of the three students called on to create the picture don't get into place, the one in the middle who was pointed to trades places with the center player.

Sidecoaching

"Commit to the picture!"

"Go to the next person!"

"Work together!"

Tips

- Once they've mastered the games, students enjoy coming up with their own ideas for new pictures and creating them.

- Over time, a group of students can develop a stock of ten, twenty, or more pictures to use in this game.

- Teach just a few new pictures at a time. Once the students have assimilated those pictures, add more.

BUS TRIP

Overview: This game is guided by the teacher and invites students to use their imagination in a series of settings and situations.

Skills that are developed include listening, following directions, empathy, self-awareness, self-confidence, and idea generation.

Instructions

- Divide the class into groups of five to eight.
- Set up chairs in a row, with sides of the chairs facing the audience.
- Bring the first group to the playing area and ask them to stand together, in front of the chairs.
- Tell the players to imagine they are at a bus stop.
- Get a suggestion from the audience about the weather.

Students learn to listen and react to each other.

- Ask the players to imagine that they are waiting for the bus in that weather.
- Tell the players that the bus is coming, but it's very far away. Guide them to watch the bus as it gets closer and to show the audience how they feel about its approach.
- Once the bus arrives, direct the players into the chairs. Coach them to be aware of the changes they feel in getting out of the weather (the bus is perfectly comfortable).
- Let the players know that this is a special bus, and they should open a special compartment in the back of the seat in front of them. Tell them there are snacks in the compartment, and they can help themselves.
- One by one, let the students tell everyone what snacks they're enjoying.
- Now that their hunger is satisfied, coach them to sit back, relax, and think about where they're going.
- Coach the players to look outside the window, still thinking about where they're going.
- One by one, focus on each student. Ask the audience how they think each student feels about where he is going.
- Then ask each student where he is going. Ask each student a few questions, such as what he will do when he gets there, who he will see, how long he will stay.

Sidecoaching

"Show us how you act when it's hot!"

"See the bus getting closer!"

"Hold the snack and look at it."

"Taste what you're eating!"

Example

Teacher: How do we think Andy feels about where he's going?

Kara: Happy.

Teacher: Happy, how?

Tai: Like something good is waiting for him.

Teacher: Where are you going, Andy?

Andy: I'm going to my friend's house.

Teacher: And why do you like going there?

Andy: He's got the best toys.

Teacher: I see. Now, how do we think Anne Marie feels about where she's going?

Peter: She looks sad.

Teacher: Where are you going, Anne Marie?

Anne Marie: To see my grandpa; he hasn't been feeling so well.

Teacher: What will you do when you see him?

Anne Marie: I'm going to try to cheer him up.

Tips

- Through sidecoaching, keep bringing players' awareness back to what they see, hear, taste, touch, and smell in the environment.
- This exercise incorporates skills developed in Space Walk and Object Work.
- This exercise is an excellent prewriting activity. After the game is finished, students can write stories about their bus trip.
- Teachers can create their own scenarios to guide students through imagination sensory details, emotions, and story events.

CONDUCTED STORY

Overview: A group of players tells a single story, led by a conductor.

Skills are developed in focus, oral communication, team building, self-confidence, and critical and creative problem solving.

Instructions

- Divide the class into small groups, five to eight players each.
- Bring the first group onstage to form a back line.
- Ask the students in the line to form a curve, and to stand close together. This arrangement helps the players listen and focus on each other.
- Ask the audience for a suggestion for the story. There are several options for this prompt:
  - Title (for example, "Dad Buys a New Used Car," "A Trip to the Mall," "The Ferris Wheel That Got Stuck")
  - Moral (examples: "Look Before You Leap," "Let the Buyer Beware," "Don't Judge a Book by Its Cover")
  - Title and genre ("The Amazing Magical Car: A Fairy Tale," "The Night My Homework Was Lost in the Graveyard: A Horror Story" "Where Did the Teachers Go?" which is a mystery)
  - Topic ("Snakes," "Cooking," "Back-to-School Shopping")
- The teacher, as the conductor, gets into position in front of the line, either sitting on a chair or kneeling. He points to one player, who then starts telling the story.
- After the player has told a portion of the story, the conductor signals to the player to stop, while pointing to another player. The new player continues the story without hesitation—even if the switch occurs in the middle of a thought, word, or sentence.
- The game continues until all students have had a couple of turns.

Sidecoaching Sidecoaching isn't recommended for Conducted Story. Players are concentrating on listening to the story, and additional words spoken by the teacher are too distracting.

Brief discussion after a round of Conducted Story can help students improve. These questions help students reflect on the game:

- Were you able to begin exactly where the last person left off? Or did you repeat the last couple of words before you continued?

- Did you get distracted? When? Why do you think you might have stopped listening?

- Did you start planning the story in your head instead of listening?

- Did the story fit the title (or topic, or moral)?

- Did you speak clearly and loudly so that the audience and the other players could hear you?

- How is this different from creating a story on your own?

Tips

- Sometimes students want to recreate movies or television programs they've seen or create stories with familiar characters. A simple, positive prompt to redirect them is "Let's get the title of a story that has never, ever been told before."

- Strong, specific movements from the conductor will help the players stay focused and know when it is their turn.

- Encourage students to tell the story in third person. This supports the idea that it is one collective story, not a first-person narrative told by whoever began the story.

- As students improve, they will tell longer, more cohesive stories. In the beginning, it's fine to keep the rounds short.

DECK OF CARDS

Overview: Students explore how nonverbal behavior gives cues about character, particularly in terms of how it relates to status.

Skills are developed in empathy, self-awareness, self-confidence, and critical and creative problem solving.

Instructions

- Divide the class into groups with anywhere from eight to eighteen players.
- Give each student a card from an ordinary deck of playing cards, with the instruction to keep the card secret from the other players.
- Tell the students to think of how the status of their card could be a character. (Example: a king could be a wealthy, powerful celebrity, and a two might be a very shy, awkward shopkeeper.)
- Tell the students to mingle and interact as though they are at a party, playing their characters.
- After several minutes, instruct the students to line up from low cards to high cards, on the basis of conclusions they've drawn from behavior at the party. Students can keep talking and interacting while they are lining up; however, they do not reveal their cards until they are all lined up.

Sidecoaching

"Keep meeting new people!"

"Does your status affect how you walk? Stand? Look at others?"

Tips

- An interesting variation is to pass out the cards with the instruction that students cannot look at their own cards. Players hold the cards in front of themselves so that others can see them. Players then draw conclusions about their status according to how others react to them.
- This exercise can open up profound discussions about status structures in school communities, including cliques, bullying, and peer pressure.
- Another variation is to create original decks of cards that are based on curriculum: for example, social classes in Ancient Greece, or characters in a novel that the class is reading.

DR. KNOW-IT-ALL

Overview: Small groups of students work together as one mind—the mind of Dr. Know-It-All—in a game that is similar to One-Word Story.

Skills are developed in listening, oral communication, team building, self-confidence, and critical and creative problem solving.

Instructions

- Set up three to eight chairs in a single row, facing forward, in the classroom playing area.
- Invite students into the playing area to sit on the chairs.
- Act as the moderator to field questions from the audience.
- Players answer the questions, each player giving just one word at a time.

Some answers may take the players two or more rounds to complete.

Sidecoaching

"Listen to each other!"

"Just say the next word!"

Instructor may also recap what has been said, or remind players of the question if they stall.

Example   (Andy, Boaz, Dina, and Sabeeha are seated in chairs.)

Teacher: We're very honored to have with us today Dr. Know-It-All, the world's leading expert on all things. Let's get a question for Dr. Know-It-All.

Nick: Dr. Know-It-All, how does a hurricane form?

Teacher: Ah, very interesting; what can you tell us about how hurricanes form, Dr. Know-It-All?

Andy: A

Boaz: hurricane

Dina: tries

Andy: Tries? That doesn't make sense.

Teacher: "A hurricane tries . . ." Go on, Sabeeha; see what you can do with that.

Sabeeha: hard.

Andy: I don't get it.

Teacher: A hurricane tries hard. . . .

Andy: to

Boaz: blow

Dina: down

Sabeeha: everything.

(Silence.)

Teacher: How does a hurricane form? Dr. Know-It-All tells us that "A hurricane tries hard to blow down everything. . . ."

Andy: because!

Boaz: it

Dina: wants

Sabeeha: to

Andy: be important.

Teacher: Thank you, Dr. Know-It-All! Remember, one word at a time. Let's try another question; we've been studying hurricanes in Science, so let's see if Dr. Know-It-All knows her facts—or if we can stump her!

Nora: What is the biggest danger when a hurricane approaches?

Andy: Storm

Boaz: surge

Dina: according

Sabeeha: to

Andy: weather

Boaz: experts.

Tips

- The teacher can take a pretty firm hand as the moderator, making sense of crazy answers, steering the audience toward specific questions, suggesting topics.

- As students become more familiar with the game, they can take turns as the moderator.

- If students are really struggling with one-word-at-a-time, it's helpful to write the words as they go somewhere they can see them. This visual reinforcement is very useful for developing the language skills necessary for this game.

- Typically, the more specific the question, the shorter the answer.

- Especially as students are first learning the game, the teacher can modify the questions for the sake of simplicity and clarity.

- Use sidecoaching to keep students on track. When students first learn this game, they may get distracted, argue with each other, and say things that don't make sense. Keep bringing their focus back to the question and what was already said.

- Allow students to make mistakes with this game. They almost always do in the beginning. If allowed to make these mistakes, they will learn much faster than if the teacher or other students jump in to fix it.

GIBBERISH

Overview: Students use a made-up language in a variety of games and scenes. There are many kinds of Gibberish exercises, and the concept is very adaptable.

Skills are developed in listening, focus, empathy, self-confidence, and critical and creative problem solving.

Instructions for Gibberish No. 1

- Divide students into pairs.
- Instruct students to take turns issuing commands to their partners. Once the partner understands the command, she can execute it. Examples would be "Wave to the teacher," "Have a seat," or "Pass the butter."

Sidecoaching

"Experiment with different sounds."

"Find new Gibberish words."

"Communicate with your partner."

"Listen to your partner."

Instructions for Gibberish No. 2

- Set up three chairs in the playing area, in a straight row facing the audience.
- Invite three students to take their places in the chairs.
- Tell them that the student in the center is a translator, and the students on either side are storytellers.
- Instruct the students on either end to tell their story, while the student in the center translates the story for the audience.

Sidecoaching

"Translate; don't invent."

"Listen to the storytellers; seek understanding."

Instructions for Gibberish No. 3

- Set up three chairs in the playing area, in a straight row facing the audience.
- Invite three students to take their places in the chairs.

- The students on either end speak different Gibberish languages and cannot understand each other. They will communicate through the student in the middle, who understands both languages.

- Choose a relationship and a point of conflict for the two players on either end that must be resolved through the translator, such as a car dealer and a customer negotiating price, two friends deciding what to have for dinner, a server trying to placate a customer who is unhappy with his meal.

Sidecoaching

"Translate; don't invent."

"Communicate; use emotion and action."

"Listen to the storytellers."

Instructions for Gibberish No. 4

- Set up two to four chairs at the front of the playing area. Chairs should be turned so that they face each other slightly.

- Invite students to take places in the chairs.

- In secret, give the students an emotion, such as fear, anger, or happiness.

- Instruct students to talk to each other in Gibberish.

- Ask the audience if they knew what the emotion was.

Sidecoaching

"Show us how you feel."

"Experiment with new sounds."

Instructions for Gibberish No. 5

- Invite three or more students into the playing area.

- In secret, give them a location such as a train station, restaurant, ice cream stand, or park.

- Instruct students to talk to each other in Gibberish, in that location.

- Ask the audience if they know what the location is.

Sidecoaching

"Show us where you are through emotion and action."

"Interact with something in the environment."

"Communicate with your partners."

Instructions for Gibberish No. 6

- Invite two players into the playing area.
- Tell them each to choose an event to relate to the other player, such as a trip to the dentist, or taking a test, or celebrating a birthday. Tell them to choose it silently, and not tell anyone.
- Instruct the players to talk to each other about their event.
- Ask each player if he understood what the other player was talking about. Ask the audience what they perceived.

Sidecoaching

"Communicate with emotion."

"Communicate with your partner."

"Listen to each other; work to understand each other."

Tips

- When first working in Gibberish, it is typical for students to try to communicate everything through elaborate miming gestures. As their ability to interpret vocal inflection and body language develops, their communication will naturally become more sophisticated.
- It's helpful to begin Gibberish work with the whole class working in pairs. Students can experiment and play with their made-up language. As their fluency in Gibberish develops, they can work with more sophisticated goals such as communicating environment, emotion, and character in Gibberish scenes.

GIVE AND TAKE

Overview: In this deceptively simple game, an ensemble works together to ensure that only one person moves at a time in the playing area. It is an extraordinarily powerful tool for team building and an excellent foundation exercise for any kind of group performance work.

Skills are developed in listening, following directions, team building, self-awareness, and self-confidence.

Instructions for Beginning Give and Take

- Invite eight to twelve students into the playing area.
- Review the boundaries of the playing area.
- Instruct students to walk freely about the playing area.
- Call out "Freeze" and "Unfreeze" until students get used to walking freely and then holding still.
- Call "Freeze" a final time. Then tell the students that you will unfreeze one student, who will then be free to walk around the group.
- Unfreeze one student with a nod or a tap on the shoulder.
- After the student has walked in and around the group for a few moments, freeze that student, and then unfreeze another. Repeat the process until every student has experienced being the only person in the group who can move.
- After the final student is frozen again, tell the students they, rather than you the teacher, will now give each other the signal to move. They will do this without touching or speaking.
- Tell the students that only one person moves at a time, and at all times one person must be moving.
- Unfreeze the first student.
- Students continue playing until everyone has moved at least once.

Sidecoaching

"Freeze completely; that means your eyes, too."

"Use the whole playing area."

"Stay alert; you could get the signal to move at any time!"

Tips for Beginning Give and Take

- When first learning to freeze, students sometimes want to strike extreme poses. Teach students the difference between freezing and posing; a freeze is simply stopping in your tracks. In addition to calling "Freeze" and "Unfreeze," call out "Pose" so that students experience the difference.
- On the same note, when students are unfrozen and moving about, they sometimes jump, stomp, dance, and so on. Introduce the concept of a "neutral walk."
- Beginners often knock into each other when they are in the process of learning this exercise. Be clear about boundaries, and give violators a brief time-out.
- At first, the moving student will stop moving and then use a strong gesture to signal that he is giving focus to a classmate to move. However, he will learn very quickly to use subtler nonverbal communication. Once the students begin to do this, sidecoaching can include "Find ways to give without eye contact" or "Keep moving until the other person starts moving."

Intermediate Give and Take

- Invite eight to twelve students into the playing area.
- Warm them up a with a quick round of beginning Give and Take.
- Tell the students they can now take the movement from each other. As soon as a frozen student begins to move, the student in motion must give up the movement and freeze.
- Remind them again that only one person moves at a time, and one person must be moving at all times.
- Play until all students have had a chance to take the movement.

Sidecoaching

"Work together; the goal of the ensemble is that only one person is moving."

"Take strong!"

"Give *and* take."

Tips

- In the beginning, it is common for two or more students to try to take at once. Go back to giving if cooperation breaks down too much, in order to give students a chance to refocus.

- If the more assertive students dominate the action, feel free to freeze them until further notice in order to give other students the opportunity to take.

- Encourage the audience to watch carefully for interesting, less obvious ways to give and take the movement.

Advanced Give and Take

- Invite eight to twelve students into the playing area.

- Warm them up with a brief round of Give and Take.

- Tell them they can now add sounds. These can be nonsense sounds, animal noises, words, short phrases, musical sounds, anything at all.

With advanced Give and Take, students can also experiment with more creative movement. They can seek different levels in the playing area, as by crawling on the floor or walking in a crouch. Using their whole body, they can experiment with fast and slow movement, movement that suggests characters, and big and small movements.

Sidecoaching

"Take strong so everyone knows you're taking!"

"Work together."

"Use the whole playing area."

Tip

- As students work more with Give and Take, they discover subtleties of emotion, pacing, and even story in the interactions between members of the ensemble.

HALF-LIFE

Overview: In this exercise, students create short scenes of two minutes and then act them out in one minute, thirty seconds, fifteen seconds, seven seconds, and three seconds.

Instructions

- Invite four students into the playing area.
- Ask the audience for characters (who), an activity (what), and a setting (where) to start the scene.
- Tell the students you will time them, and at exactly two minutes you will stop them.
- After they have improvised for two minutes, tell them to redo the exact same scene in half the time (one minute).
- Repeat the scene at thirty seconds, then at fifteen seconds, then seven, then three.

Sidecoaching

"What happened next?"

"You have _____ seconds left!"

"Show us as much as you can!"

Tips

- It doesn't matter if the first two-minute scene is disjointed. Part of the joy of this exercise is that it helps students get to the point. The half-life process often helps clarify the scene.
- This is a very high-energy game. If focus starts to waver, move to another exercise and tell the students they can return to this exercise once they're refocused.
- As students become more comfortable performing improvised scenes, introduce useful dialogue guidelines that help keep the scene moving forward:
  - Make statements rather than ask questions, because questions have a way of bogging down a scene ("Where are you going?" "What are you doing?" "Why are we here?" all throw responsibility onto the other person in the scene). Avoiding questions supports each player in making bold, specific choices, which keep the scene vital.
  - "Yes, and . . .": agree with and support what's happening in the scene.

MIRROR

Overview: Pairs of students face each other and work together to mirror each other's movements.

Skills are developed in focus, empathy, self-awareness, and self-confidence.

Instructions

- Calling students up in pairs assigned by the teacher, bring either the whole class or half of the class into the playing area, depending on how much space is available.

- If the class has an odd number of students, three students can work together.

- Instruct the pairs of students to face each other.

- Tell the students to decide who is A and who is B in each pair.

- Tell the students that A is a person looking into a mirror, and that B is the image in that mirror.

These boys concentrate as they participate in "mirror."

- Instruct B to mirror A—posture, facial expression, breathing, arms folded, standing with more weight on one leg, and so on.
- On the teacher's signal, A may begin to move slowly as B follows.
- At any point, call "Freeze" and bring the attention of the class to one pair, asking, "Can you tell which one is the mirror?"
- Switch A to the mirror and B to the person looking in the mirror so that students can experience both sides of the exercise.

Sidecoaching

"Work together; we shouldn't be able to tell who's following and who's leading."

"Use your whole body."

"Use your faces."

"Support your mirror to follow you."

Tips

- Sometimes pairs of students try to trick each other, with the partner looking in the mirror deliberately trying to trick the mirror into making a mistake. Focusing on each pair and asking the audience if they can tell who is the mirror is a way to redirect their focus. Instead of tricking each other, they should be working together to trick the *audience.*
- Once students become adept at this exercise, pairs can switch roles at random, without prompting from the teacher.

OBJECT WORK

Overview: Object work is a broad term that denotes creating objects with mime techniques.

Skills are developed in focus, self-awareness, self-confidence, idea generation, and critical and creative problem solving.

Instructions

- Students can do this exercise at their desks.
- Tell students they are surrounded by space, and they can move their arms and hands through it quite easily because it is empty.
- Now, tell the students to move their hands forward until they feel a brick wall. Tell them to explore the brick wall with their hands, feeling the texture, temperature.
- Ask the students to tell you how the wall feels.
- Now, tell them to take their hands away from the wall.
- Tell the students to move their hands forward again until they reach a wall made of Jell-o. Tell them to squish their hands into it and move them around.
- Ask the students to tell you how it feels, how it smells.
- Tell them to grab a hunk and taste it. Ask them how it tastes.
- Tell them to take their hands out; it's time to wash them. They can pick up their favorite soap, smell it, lather up, rinse their hands, and dry them. Don't forget to shut off the faucet!

Other Ideas for Beginner Exercises

- Create a basketball (or softball, or football) out of thin air. Toss it up and down, score goals, bounce it against the ceiling, throw it up through the ceiling and into the sky above the school, throw it all the way into outer space, and let it fall back into the classroom again.
- Pull a present out of thin air and open it. Each student decides how big the package is and whether to tear the wrapping off quickly or carefully, and picks up the object. Students can explain what they received.
- Eating and drinking: guided by the teacher's instructions, students can enjoy object-work pizza, popcorn, milk and cookies, and other food or drink.

More Advanced Object Work

- Students can do this in their chairs, or move into a large circle. This exercise works best with the whole class participating at once.

- The first person, either a student or the teacher, holds an imaginary object, feels it, uses it, and then passes it to the next person.

- This next person takes the object, and begins to feel its weight, size, texture. As he does so, the object begins to change in his hands. He reacts to the new dimensions of the object until the transformation is complete and then passes it to the next person.

- The process is repeated until all students have experienced it.

Example   Tammy holds a small object in both hands. She then grasps one end in her fist and runs the other end on her open palm. She looks at the object, and then brings it to her head and starts stroking it across her hair. She passes it to Corey. He grasps it in his fist also, but it seems to grow heavier. As he pats the object against an open palm, it gets longer and longer until he grips it on one end with both fists. He taps one end on the ground, sets his feet wider and brings the object up to his shoulders in a baseball batter's stance. He then passes the object to Ibro, who holds it in one hand, feeling the weight. It gets lighter, and as he runs a hand across the changing object, it gets much thinner. He swings it back and forth in one hand, and then cranks a small wheel at one end of it.

Creating an Environment with Objects: Instructions

- Invite up to eight players into the playing space to get into a back line.

- In secret, help them choose a location.

- One by one, each player comes out and interacts with an object in the environment. More than one student can interact with the same object.

- The audience guesses the environment through the clues of the environment.

Example   Ellie steps out of the back line and looks through a rack of clothes. Milla joins her and they hold up outfits on hangers in front of themselves and each other. Taishan comes out of the back line and stands, taking objects from a counter in front of him, looking at them, punching numbers into a machine, and placing the objects behind him. Corey enters the scene and stands by

Taishan, swiping a credit card in a reader and punching in numbers. Juan enters and stands by Corey, pulling items off a rack and putting them on the counter for Taishan to ring up. Marie enters, pushing a cart; she pulls items out of the cart and puts them on shelves. The audience guesses that they are in a store.

Sidecoaching

"What does that feel (taste, smell, sound, look) like?"

"How heavy (light) is that?"

"Feel that object in your hand; hold it!"

"Don't show us the object; react to it."

Tips

- Object work can be a great warm-up writing exercise.
- Younger students usually enjoy object-work exercises for their own sake, but sometimes older students need a stronger context or goal in order not to feel self-conscious with object work.
- Always encourage students to be as specific as possible; for example, if they're eating pizza, ask them if it's deep-dish or thin-crust. If they're creating a store, ask them if it's a grocery store or a hardware store.

ONE-WORD STORY

Overview: In this exercise, players tell a story one word at a time.

Skills are developed in listening, focus, oral communication, team building, self-confidence, and critical and creative problem solving.

Instructions

- Students can play this either at their desks or in a back-line formation of up to eight players. If the back line is used, it's helpful to curve the line so that the students are better able to focus on each other.

- Instruct the students that they will tell one story, as a group, with each student providing one word at a time.

- Tell the students that this is a story no one has ever heard before, with characters no one has ever seen.

- In the first few rounds, the teacher can prompt each student by pointing. As students become more adept at the exercise, they can take their turns without prompting.

- Optional add-ons:

  - Begin with a title for the story to keep the students focused.

  - Name the characters and setting before the story begins.

  - At the end of the story, tell the moral of the story, one word at a time.

  - Assign a style for the story, such as thriller, fable, action adventure, or others.

Sidecoaching

"Nice and loud!"

"Listen to each other."

"Support the story."

"Help tie it together."

"Make sense out of it!"

"One word only."

"Quiet; focus; listen to all of the words."

Tips

- Writing the words down on a flip chart or chalkboard helps students achieve fluency.

- In the beginning, as they are learning, students may freeze or get stuck. Repeat the story they have created so far. If the teacher is writing down the story, he can ask a student to read what has been created to that point.

- It is imperative to let students make mistakes with this exercise; do not rush in to save them if they struggle. If they say something that doesn't make sense, write it down and move on. Once the round is completed, read it back and let the students hear it. They will learn to listen to each other to achieve the goals of this exercise much more quickly than if the teacher corrects them midstory.

- In the first few rounds, let it take as long as it needs to take, which could be a long time.

- If a student jumps in to supply a word for another student who hesitates, that student forfeits his next turn.

Example of Beginner's Round

Tom: My

Frankie: brother

Nora: sister

Ellie: That doesn't make sense.

Teacher: Let's see if we can make it work.

Ellie: But it doesn't make sense, brother, sister—

Teacher: Listen: My brother, sister. . . .

Ellie: mother

Milla: and

Dina: me

Boaz: went

Ranjit: store

Nora: uh—

Teacher: One word.

Nora: I don't know.

Ellie: Shopping!

Wei: It's not your turn.

Teacher: That's right; it's Nora's turn. My brother, sister, mother, and me went store—

Nora: to buy

Teacher: One word.

Nora: to

Corey: buy

Tom: something

Frankie: bicycle.

Example of Advanced Round

Marco: James

Nick: Weatherby

Raneesha: Junior

Kate: woke

Ciera: up

Samara: early

Andy: because

Jessica: barking

Gabriela: outside

Andy: no—barking was—

Teacher: woke up early because barking outside; make it work, Mohamed

Mohamed: her

Dionna: house

Corey: was

Dina: loud.

PANEL OF EXPERTS

Overview: In this exercise, a group plays a panel of experts to explore point of view and character.

Skills are developed in oral communication, team building, self-awareness, self-confidence, critical and creative problem solving, and idea generation.

Instructions

- Invite three to six players into the playing area.
- Players sit in chairs facing the audience.
- The teacher assigns an area of expertise for each member on the panel. One of the traditional ways to do this is to ask the audience simple questions and use the answers as the area of expertise. (See example.)
- Ask each expert to introduce herself with a character name, and a brief statement about her area of expertise.
- The host asks the panel questions and prompts each expert to answer in turn.
- After a couple of questions, the audience may ask questions.

Example

Teacher: All right; who can tell me their least favorite chore?

Audience member: Taking out the garbage.

Teacher: Excellent. Tim, you are an expert in garbage, in waste management. Who can tell me their favorite pastime?

Audience member: Video games.

Teacher: Excellent. Sameera, you are an expert in video games.

Sameera: I don't know anything about video games.

Teacher: Name one.

Sameera: Rollercoaster Tycoon.

Teacher: You know enough to pretend you are an expert. And who can tell me what they did this weekend?

Audience member: Missed my soccer game because of the thunderstorm.

Teacher: Great. Carrie, you're an expert in thunderstorms. Let me start by asking the panel to introduce themselves—and please tell us a little bit about your credentials, if you would be so kind.

Tim: Hi. I'm Oscar Trash and I'm the bestest, smelliest, hardest-working garbage man in this town.

Sameera: Hi; I'm Ms. Gamer, and I love video games.

Carrie: I'm Alexandra Lightning. I bet you've seen me on Channel 5000 giving you the weather. I know everything about weather.

Teacher: Great! Well, we're very happy to have you all here today. Let me start off the questions. Panel, what's the best kind of exercise to get?

Tim: I'll be glad to answer that. The best exercise is the kind that makes the most waste. Disposable baseball bats, balls, and bases, I love them. Paper uniforms. You can just tear them off and throw them away when you're done. I'll be glad to take care of the rest.

Teacher: Thank you. Ms. Gamer?

Sameera: I don't believe in exercise. Unless it's those little guys jumping around on the screen. Let them do all the work.

Teacher: I see. Alexandra?

Carrie: Any outdoor activities; they're all excellent as long as you remember to check the weather reports and prepare for any weather. A big coat if it's the winter, and bring lots of water if it's hot. And find something else to do if it's a big storm. You could get knocked over in the wind, and that's not really exercise. It's just falling down.

Tips

- After students are familiar with the game, a student can act as the host.

- This exercise adapts well to using specific curriculum content: experts in systems of the body, experts in periods of history, and so on. Experts can also be famous scientists or characters in a novel.

PARTS OF A WHOLE

Overview: In this exercise, students work together to create a variety of locations, objects, animals, machines, or anything else they can dream up.

Skills are developed in listening, team building, self-awareness, self-confidence, critical and creative problem solving, and idea generation.

Instructions

- Invite six to ten students into a back line.

- The teacher and the audience select something to create.

- One student steps out of the back line and announces what part of the whole he will become.

- The student becomes that part with his whole body.

- The next student steps out and announces what part she will become.

- She adds onto the whole by becoming her part.

- The exercise continues until all students have stepped out of the back line.

- Optional add-ons:

  - Brainstorm the parts of the whole before the exercise begins. This is particularly helpful for English language learners and younger children. It aids in vocabulary building and conceptualization of the final object.

  - Let the audience provide the parts; the students on stage simply embody them.

- Once the whole is completed, ask the students to put it into sound and motion (for example, a car revving up and moving forward, an elephant roaring and swinging its trunk, a tree rustling and swaying in the breeze, or other ideas).

Example

Teacher: We need any kind of thing to create here. What do you want to see?

Audience member: A computer.

Teacher: OK, we're going to make a computer.

Davis: I'm the computer.

Teacher: Which part?

Davis: The computer part.

Teacher: The monitor, where you see the picture?

Davis: Yeah.

Teacher: OK, Davis, be the monitor.

(Davis stands as the monitor, hands at sides.)

Teacher: What shape is that computer screen? Can you show us?

(Davis makes a square shape with his arms.)

Kara: I'm the keyboard.

(She sits on the floor and sticks her hands out, mimes typing.)

Teacher: Are you the keyboard, or the person typing at the keyboard?

Kara: Oh! I'm the keyboard.

(She lays down flat on the floor.)

Samara: I'll be the mouse.

(She sits on the floor next to Kara.)

Jim: All the parts are taken, now.

Teacher: We have the monitor, the keyboard, the mouse; what else can be part of this computer?

(Students left on the back line are blank.)

Teacher: Can some of the parts have parts?

Jim: Oh! I'll be the screensaver!

(He stands behind the square Davis made with his arms and wiggles his hands.)

Teacher: Great! What else?

Sidecoaching

"Work together!"

"Show us what that looks like!"

"What part is connected to what we already see?"

"What's missing?"

Tips

- It might take a while before students are comfortable physicalizing the parts. As they grow more secure with the exercise and each other, they have more fun embodying the parts. Their work also becomes more specific.
- If students are really struggling with the concept of physicalizing the parts, jump in and model physicalization for them; then step out and let them do it for themselves.

PASS THE CLAP

Overview: This exercise is often used as a warm-up and is excellent for building an ensemble. Students work together to pass a handclap around a circle.

Skills are developed in following directions, focus, team building, self-awareness, and self-confidence.

Instructions

- Invite students to create a circle. Even in a large class, the entire group can participate in the exercise at the same time.
- Instruct students that they will pass a clap around the circle.
- Begin with two students: instruct them to face each other and clap at the same time.
- The student on the left then turns and faces a new partner. Again, they clap at the same time.
- Repeat until the clap has passed around the circle at least once.

Sidecoaching

"Work together!"

"Make eye contact!"

"Each pair of claps should make just one sound."

Tips

- This is another game that is deceptively simple. If students are having trouble clapping simultaneously, try this demonstration: ask several pairs of students to face other. Instruct them to look at each other's hands and clap. Then, instruct them to look into each other's eyes and clap. Almost always, looking into a partner's eyes is more effective.
- Sometimes students, excited by the game, want to speed up the exercise. Especially as they are learning how to play, this can cause the game to get sloppy. Stop them, point out what's happening, and encourage them to slow down and work together.

- Once they have mastered the basic exercise, some variations can add challenge:

  - Reversing the clap: the player receiving the clap can remain facing the player who passed the clap, clap again, and send the clap back around the circle in the other direction.

  - More claps: the teacher or one of the student players can introduce another clap into the circle, so that more than one clap is circulating at once.

  - Throwing it across the circle: a receiver may elect to pass the clap to any of the players in the circle.

SLIDE SHOW

Overview: Two groups of students work together to create a slide show for the audience. One group forms the pictures, and the other group furnishes descriptions and background on the pictures.

Skills are developed in oral communication, team building, and self-confidence.

Instructions

- Invite two students up to the playing area; instruct them to stand or sit in chairs to one side of the playing area. These students are the narrators.
- Invite five to eight students into the playing area. These students create the slides.
- Instruct students to come the center of the playing area, one at a time, and freeze. Tell them to find different playing levels: high, medium, and low. They can sit, stand, lie on the ground, or get into any other position.
- Ask the audience to suggest a location for a vacation.
- The two students on the sidelines then explain to the audience what the "slide" is all about.

Either the students or the teacher can call "Next" for a new slide. At that point, the entire slide group moves into a new frozen pose.

Sidecoaching

"Work together so we can see everyone!"

"Find new levels!"

"Show us how you feel!"

Tips

- Vacation slides are an excellent starting point to learn the exercise, but this exercise is infinitely adaptable. Students can create and explain slides of the solar system, Arctic expeditions, Civil War action, or other places or events.
- These instructions call for the slide group to initiate, but the exercise can easily be played with the narrators initiating. They can give a brief explanation of what the audience will see in the slide, and give the cue to the slide players to create the picture.

Explanation of Improvisation Exercises   **89**

- A traditional version of this exercise calls for each player to be in physical contact with at least one other player. This tends to promote much stronger stage pictures, and most students who have been working with improvisation games understand the boundaries of appropriate physical contact.
- As students are learning, it can be very useful for the teacher to sit with the narrating students to suggest ideas and ask prompting questions.

Example

> Teacher: OK, we have the suggestion of an activity: "Building Our Tree House." Let's take a look at the first slide.
>
> (Students get into position.)
>
> Sayeed: Oh, this is when my dad got back from the lumber yard.
>
> Carrie: He stepped on a nail; that's him on the ground there.
>
> Sayeed: Yeah, and the rest of the crew didn't even notice.
>
> Teacher: They don't look like they're doing much work yet.
>
> Carrie: It was a really beautiful day.
>
> Teacher: Let's see another slide; next!
>
> (Students move into another position.)
>
> Teacher: Find a new level. Discover what you are doing in this group of people building a tree house.
>
> Sayeed: Oh! That's my mom helping my dad get the nail out of his foot.
>
> Carrie: And that's your little brother; he's laughing!
>
> Sayeed: That's what he does.
>
> Teacher: What's happening here?
>
> Carrie: Oh, those guys are measuring wood for the tree house.

SPACE WALK

Overview: This basic, adaptable exercise offers wonderful opportunities to imagine, visualize, explore, and discover through kinesthetic learning.

Skills are developed in focus, following directions, self-awareness, and self-confidence.

Instructions

- Invite any number from ten students to the entire class into the playing area, as space will allow.
- Instruct students to walk through the space.
- While they are walking, keep talking to the students so that they become accustomed to keeping one part of their focus on listening to instructions while the rest of their focus is on the exercise.

Students listen to directions as they explore their space.

- Remind the students to move throughout the entire playing area and to move in a random pattern.

These are the basic instructions. Here are just a few variations:

- Instruct students to freeze and unfreeze.
- Tell them to walk as though the floor is covered with sticky goo; ask them to walk through syrup, through mud, or on a sandy beach.
- Instruct students to walk ankle deep in water, knee deep in water, waist deep, chest deep.
- Have the students "try on" several kinds of shoes: athletic shoes, wheelies, ice skates, boots, high heels.
- Ask the students to walk as though they were different ages: three, twenty-one, forty, eighty.
- Emotion walks: have the students walk like someone who is happy, sad, angry, and so on.
- Contact or no contact: give students a variety of ways to contact each other as they pass, such as eye contact, a nod, a wave, hello, deliberately looking away, frowning. In between types of contact, ask them to go back to no contact to develop their awareness of the difference.
- Stage focus: when students freeze, give them an additional instruction that is a point of focus, such as "Freeze—focus center," "Freeze—focus on Jerry," or "Freeze—focus outside of this room."
- Speed up and slow down: tell the students that on a scale of one to ten they are currently moving at a four or a five. Coach them into speeding up to ten and slowing down to one.
- Status walk: divide the group into two parts. Instruct students to make eye contact as they pass each other. Instruct one of the groups to hold eye contact and the other group to break eye contact as soon as they can while they pass. Then ask the groups to switch eye contact roles.
- Leading with body parts: ask students to move through the space, leading with their nose, their shoulders, their chest, their head, and other body parts.
- Curriculum exploration: space walks can be designed to explore characters in a book, environments, emotions, historical figures, and so on.

Sidecoaching

"Stay in motion."

"Explore the whole space."

"Feel your feet make contact with the floor, the air moving over your body."

"Feel your body moving in the space."

"Listen to me and stay in the exercise at the same time."

"Look for a space that needs to be filled, and move to it."

Tips

- Even advanced students who have done a lot of work with Space Walks benefit by starting with the simplest version of the exercise as a warm-up: simply moving through the space and focusing on their body.

- This is an excellent writing exercise warm-up, especially for those kinesthetically oriented students who are easily blocked.

- Invite students to explore and appreciate the differences between a neutral walk and a walk with an added element (such as age, or leading with a body part, or walking through water.) This helps their overall focus in the exercise.

STRING OF PEARLS

Overview: In this game, a group of students create a story one sentence at a time.

Skills are developed in focus, listening, oral communication, self-confidence, critical and creative problem solving, and idea generation.

Instructions

- Invite eight to twelve students to form a back line.
- Tell students they are going to create an original story, one that has never been told before. Each student will contribute one sentence for this story.
- Ask a student to offer a beginning line for the story. Instruct that student to step forward and take the first position in the story line.
- Ask a student to give a final line for the story. Instruct that student to step forward and take the last position in the story line.
- Tell the remaining students that they can fill in a sentence *any place on the line.* They do not have to fall into the line one after another.
- Each time a student takes her place in the line, the story is retold from the very beginning. This helps the students track the story.

Sidecoaching

"Step into the line and help the story."

"Just say the first thing you think of."

"Find a gap in the story and fill it."

Example

Teacher: OK, who wants to give us the first line of our story? Sameera? Excellent. What is the first line?

Sameera: There was a princess who wanted her own dragon more than anything else in the world.

Teacher: Very nice. Who wants to give us that last line? Tom—good—get into place, and we'll start from the beginning. Sameera?

Sameera: There was a princess who wanted her own dragon more than anything else in the world.

Tom: The castle lay in a smoking pile of ruins.

Teacher: OK, now anyone else may step in.

(Dina steps into the story line.)

Sameera: There was a princess who wanted her own dragon more than anything else in the world.

Dina: The dragon had a terrible temper.

Tom: The castle lay in a smoking pile of ruins.

(Sean steps into the story line between Dina and Tom.)

Sean: The king said the castle was too small for a dragon, but the princess wanted her way.

Teacher: Great. But let's hear the story from the beginning.

Sameera: There was a princess who wanted her own dragon more than anything else in the world.

Dina: The dragon had a terrible temper.

Sean: The king said the castle was too small for a dragon, but the princess wanted her way.

Tom: The castle lay in a smoking pile of ruins.

(Diwonne steps into the story line between Sameera and Dina.)

Teacher: Great; from the beginning now, and Diwonne will jump in when we get to his part.

Sameera: There was a princess who wanted her own dragon more than anything else in the world.

Diwonne: So she carefully saved her allowance until she was able to buy one all by herself.

Dina: The dragon had a terrible temper.

Sean: The king said the castle was too small for a dragon, but the princess wanted her way.

Tom: The castle lay in a smoking pile of ruins.

Teacher: Excellent. Who is next?

(Cooper steps into the story line between Sean and Tom.)

Sameera: There was a princess who wanted her own dragon more than anything else in the world.

Diwonne: So she carefully saved her allowance until she was able to buy one all by herself.

Dina: The dragon had a terrible temper.

Sean: The king said the castle was too small for a dragon, but the princess wanted her way.

Cooper: So the princess had her birthday party at the laser tag place.

Tom: The castle lay in a smoking pile of ruins.

Dina: This doesn't make sense now! Cooper ruined it!

Teacher: Nothing's ruined. We just have an unexpected twist—something every good story has. Let's see if we can get it to make sense. Next?

(Angelique steps into the story line between Dina and Sean.)

Sameera: There was a princess who wanted her own dragon more than anything else in the world.

Diwonne: So she carefully saved her allowance until she was able to buy one all buy herself.

Dina: The dragon had a terrible temper.

Angelique: So the princess couldn't invite him to her fancy birthday party at the laser tag place, and she told her father that the dragon could stay home in the castle.

Sean: The king said the castle was too small for a dragon, but the princess wanted her way.

Cooper: So the princess had her birthday party at the laser tag place.

Tom: The castle lay in a smoking pile of ruins.

Teacher: Well done! And last but not least, Ibro?

(Ibro steps into the story line between Cooper and Tom.)

Sameera: There was a princess who wanted her own dragon more than anything else in the world.

Diwonne: So she carefully saved her allowance until she was able to buy one all by herself.

Dina: The dragon had a terrible temper.

Angelique: So the princess couldn't invite him to her fancy birthday party at the laser tag place, and she told her father that the dragon could stay home in the castle.

Sean: The king said the castle was too small for a dragon, but the princess wanted her way.

Cooper: So the princess had her birthday party at the laser tag place.

Ibro: And the dragon stayed in the castle, where his bad temper got the better of him and by the end of the day—

Tom: The castle lay in a smoking pile of ruins.

Final order of the line:

Sameera	Diwonne	Dina	Angelique	Sean	Cooper	Ibro	Tom
1	5	3	7	4	6	8	2

Tips

- When students first learn this game, they typically fall into place one after the other. Once they get more comfortable playing, they become more playful with the sequencing.

- When students are learning, it is extremely helpful to write the sentences where everyone can see them so that students can track the story.

- The first few rounds may be slow, and the stories may not make sense. Students quickly learn how to work together to create a satisfying story.

- Many teachers have used this exercise as a written exercise. One great variation is to set out index cards or strips of paper next to an empty bulletin board. As students finish assignments or transition to one activity or another, they can be invited to write out a sentence and post it on the bulletin board. By the end of the day, the class will have completed a story that can be shared.

- A variation is to begin with one sentence that will be the middle of the story. The students then build out the story line, adding a sentence at the beginning, then at the end, and alternating until all students are in place:

  8   6   4   2   1   3   5   7   9

TAKE THAT BACK

Overview: This game is based in simple scenes. A moderator interrupts the scene periodically with the command to "take that back" so that players have to come up with alternative lines of dialogue.

Skills are developed in listening, focus, oral communication, critical and creative problem solving, and idea generation.

Instructions

- Invite two to four students into the playing area.

- Ask the audience for characters (who), an activity (what), and a setting (where) to start the scene.

- At key points, the teacher claps and calls out "Take that back!" and the last player who spoke must generate a new line of dialogue. Repeat this with the same player until three new lines of dialogue have been generated.

- Continue the scene until everyone has had the opportunity to generate new lines of dialogue.

Sidecoaching

"Say the first thing you think of!"

"Stay in the scene!"

"Look at your partner and react!"

Tips

- Sustained scenes require fairly advanced improvisation skills to execute effectively, but this simple scenic exercise is much easier for new improvisers and is an excellent way to introduce scene work.

- As students become more comfortable performing improvised scenes, introduce useful dialogue guidelines that help keep the scene moving forward:

  - Make statements rather than ask questions; questions have a way of bogging down a scene ("Where are you going?" "What are you doing?" "Why are we here?" throw responsibility onto the other person in the scene).

  - Avoiding questions supports each player in making bold, specific choices, which keep the scene vital.

- "Yes, and . . .": agree with and support what's happening in the scene.

Example

Teacher: OK, our "who" is four siblings, our activity ("what") is making breakfast, and our "where" is the family question. Go ahead and start.

Boaz: I want cornflakes.

Jessica: I'm going to make waffles. And you can't stop me.

Blaine: Jessica, you know Mom and Dad aren't home.

Teacher: Take that back.

Blaine: Jessica, you know that you're not supposed to use the waffle iron.

Teacher: Take that back!

Blaine: Jessica, you're going to burn the house down.

Teacher: Take that back!

Blaine: I'll get the waffle mix.

Wendy: You guys! Mom and Dad said don't use anything electrical.

Boaz: I'm just having cornflakes. So I won't be in trouble.

Teacher: Take that back!

Boaz: I'm just having cornflakes. And I'm telling on Blaine and Jessica.

Teacher: Take that back!

Boaz: I'd have cornflakes, so I wouldn't get in trouble, but it seems we're out.

Teacher: Take that back!

Boaz: I'm going to watch TV. Tell me if you need me to call the fire department.

Mark: Looks like the cord on this waffle iron is kind of frayed.

THROWING LIGHT

Overview: In this exercise, students must use clues to figure out a topic of conversation.

Skills are developed in listening, focus, oral communication, self-confidence, critical and creative problem solving, and idea generation.

Instructions

- Invite anywhere from ten students to the entire class into the playing area. Space permitting, the students can form a back line.
- Choose two players to decide, in secret, on a topic of conversation.
- Tell the students to discuss the topic in front of everyone, but they cannot specifically mention what they are discussing.
- As soon as another player knows the topic, he can join in the conversation.

The original players may ask the newcomer to whisper the topic to them. If the newcomer is wrong, he has to step back out.

Sidecoaching

"Share your voice."

"Explore your topic without mentioning it by name."

Example

Teacher: OK, Katie and Mary: pick a topic and go.

Katie: It's one of my favorite things in the world.

Mary: Me too. But I have to be careful how much I do it or I have problems.

Katie: When I go someplace, I really like to check out the local versions.

Mary: Me too! Canada has good ones.

Katie: It's fun to get enough to share.

Mary: My grandmother would always get a lot and share it. She liked big fancy boxes of it.

(Richard joins the conversation.)

Richard: My dentist would prefer I change my habits.

Mary: You got a lot of cavities?

Richard: Yeah.

   (Michaela joins the conversation.)

Michaela: I do it every night, last thing before I go to bed.

Katie: Tell me what you think it is, Michaela.

   (Michaela whispers "brushing your teeth" and has to sit back down.)

Richard: My dentist told me to brush afterwards, but if I don't have my tooth-
   brush with me, well. . . .

   (Jaime joins the conversation.)

Jaime: I love that every couple of months, there's a holiday that gives you permission to go crazy with it.

Katie: Yeah. Halloween is the big one.

   (Michaela comes back in.)

Michaela: My mom told me I couldn't do it before meals.

   (Students continue until they all join the conversation about "eating candy.")

Tips

- When students are learning this game, it is helpful for teachers to participate with the students in order to model how to discuss the topic without
  naming it.

- This game is excellent for developing skills in inferencing and synthesizing
  information.

- Some students have a lot of difficulty with this game, especially when first
  learning it. When the teacher plays along, he can help struggling students with
  more pointed conversational clues.

WHO STARTED THE MOTION?

Overview: In this simple exercise, students work together to conceal the identity of the person initiating motions. It is a good warm-up and helps students focus on each other and working together.

Skills are developed in following directions, team building, self-awareness, and self-confidence.

Instructions

- Invite at least six students or up to the whole class to stand in a circle in the playing area.
- Choose one student to leave the room for just a few seconds.
- Select a student in the circle to be the leader.
- The leader begins a repetitive movement (such as snapping fingers, shaking hands, patting head) and everyone in the circle imitates that movement.

The student who left the room returns and either stands in the center of the circle or joins the circle and has three guesses to figure out who is leading the motion.

Sidecoaching

"Work together so no one can tell who is leading!"

"Don't give it away with your eyes!"

"Go ahead and guess!"

Tips

A variation of this game can be played with students sitting at their desks. Eliminate the guessing element by having the teacher simply choose students to be the motion leaders without stopping in between. Played this way, it gives the teacher a very efficient visual diagnostic of how well each student in the class is listening and focused.

ZIP ZAP ZOP

Overview: In this fast-paced game of concentration, students pass energy and focus to each other.

Skills are developed in listening, following directions, focus, and self-confidence.

Instructions

- Invite anywhere from six students up to the entire class to stand in a circle in the playing area.
- The first time the game is played, ask all of the students to practice an "energy clap," in which they sweep one hand across the other and end up pointing their whole hand toward another player. Done correctly, this brush-clap will make a clapping sound.
- Once they've mastered the energy clap, tell them to accompany each clap by saying "Zip" or "Zap" or "Zop."
- Tell students that "zip zap zop" is a mutating ball of energy that will change every time it moves to another player, from zip to zap to zop and then back to zip again.
- To begin the game, one student claps at someone and says "Zip." The receiver claps at someone else and says "Zop," and so forth.

A new round begins when someone doesn't receive or send, or gets "zip zap zop" out of sequence.

Sidecoaching

"Make eye contact. Agree that you are sending and receiving."

"Focus is more important than speed."

"Keep the energy in motion."

Tips

- Eye contact is very important in this exercise. Remind students to make eye contact with each other before passing the energy.

- Students enjoy playing elimination rounds; when someone drops the energy, he sits out.

- In large classes, three, four, or more circles can be set up at the same time to play the game.

Reference

Spolin, V. (1986). *Improvisation for the theater* (3rd ed.). Evanston, IL: Northwestern University Press.

Skills and Teaching

This chapter consists of lessons from K–8 teachers in the United States and Canada. All of the teachers who created these lesson plans were trained in Second City education programs and are actively using improvisation as a teaching tool in their classrooms. Each lesson is aligned to McREL (Mid-Continent Research for Education and Learning) and Ontario Curriculum Ministry standards that demonstrate each teacher's keen ability to use improvisation for creative teaching and learning. We are grateful to all of the teachers who contributed lessons for this book.

IMPROVISATIONAL ACTIVITY USED IN THIS LESSON: AD GAME

Lesson: Lights, Camera . . . Re-Action!

Grade level: sixth to eighth grade

Subject: reading and language arts or drama

Time length for lesson: twenty minutes for improv; two class periods for follow-up written assignment and oral presentation

Valerie Lowry Murray, a teacher from Barrington, Illinois, authored this lesson.

Lesson Overview   On reading a class novel, short story, or play, students demonstrate awareness of what they read by improvising as though they are talent agents. They cast components of the reading into a movie by citing modern celebrities to play the characters, direct the movie, and compose music for the production. Students will use the format of the Second City Ad Game to react to

Students share movements in Give and Take exercise.

the reading. After the movie has been cast, students formulate the ad department, which will launch the campaign for the movie.

Student Learning Objectives Students will use ensemble skills to review critical elements of what has been read. This serves as a review of the content.

Instructional Plan and Explanation of Learning Activities

Step One: Students pinpoint characters, plot development, and author's theme by transferring these elements into a modern cinematic showcase. This can be completed through a large-group class discussion or in small discussion groups.

Step Two: Through improvisation, students determine the casting of actors, select music to enhance various scenes in the reading, hire a director, and contract an ad agency to spotlight the movie.

Step Three: Students demonstrate ensemble skills as they focus as a group on what was read and transition that into the final creative outlet.

Assessment Plan for Lesson The students' oral presentation and written ad can be evaluated with this rubric.

Additional Comments and Tips from the Teacher This gives a wonderful means to reinforce what has been read, as well as prepare for any final test on the novel, short story, or play. Students are able to take more ownership in their learning when they are an integral part of what is being taught.

Subject: Reading and Language Arts Drama
Lesson: Lights, Camera, Re-Action!

Grade Level	McREL Standards	Ontario Curriculum Ministry Expectations
6	6. Uses reading skills and strategies to understand and interpret a variety of literary texts 8. Uses listening and speaking strategies for various purposes 10. Understands the characteristics and components of the media	**Reading** **Demonstrating understanding** **1.4** Demonstrate understanding of increasingly complex texts by summarizing and explaining important ideas, and citing relevant supporting details **Making inferences, interpreting texts** **1.5** Develop interpretations about texts using stated and implied ideas to support their interpretations **Extending understanding** **1.6** Extend understanding of texts by connecting, comparing, and contrasting the ideas in them to their own knowledge, experience, and insights, to other familiar texts, and to the world around them **Interconnected skills** **4.2** Explain, in conversation with the teacher and/or peers or in a reader's notebook, how their skills in listening, speaking, writing, viewing, and representing help them make sense of what they read
7		**Reading** **Demonstrating understanding** **1.4** Demonstrate understanding of increasingly complex texts by summarizing important ideas and citing a variety of details that support the main idea

Grade Level	McREL Standards	Ontario Curriculum Ministry Expectations
		Making inferences, interpreting texts
		1.5 Develop and explain interpretations of increasingly complex or difficult texts using stated and implied ideas from the texts to support their interpretations
		Extending understanding
		1.6 Extend understanding of texts, including increasingly complex or difficult texts, by connecting the ideas in them to their own knowledge, experience, and insights, to other familiar texts, and to the world around them
8		**Reading**
		Demonstrating understanding
		1.4 Demonstrate understanding of increasingly complex texts by summarizing important ideas and citing a variety of details that support the main idea
		Making inferences, interpreting texts
		1.5 Develop and explain interpretations of increasingly complex or difficult texts using stated and implied ideas from the texts to support their interpretations
		Extending understanding
		1.6 Extend understanding of texts, including increasingly complex or difficult texts, by connecting the ideas in them to their own knowledge, experience, and insights, to other familiar texts, and to the world around them

Assessment Rubric for Lights, Camera. . . Re-Action!

Written Portion of Assignment

Category	4	3	2	1
Topic focus	The ad is related to the assigned topic and allows the reader to understand much more about the topic.	Most of the ad is related to the assigned topic. The story wanders off at one point, but the reader can still learn something about the topic.	Some of the ad is related to the assigned topic, but the reader does not learn much about the topic.	No attempt has been made to relate the ad to the assigned topic.
Creativity	The ad contains many creative details or descriptions that contribute to the reader's enjoyment.	The ad contains a few creative details or descriptions that contribute to the reader's enjoyment.	The ad contains a few creative details or descriptions, but they distract from the story.	There is little evidence of creativity in the ad.

Oral Portion of Assignment

Category	4	3	2	1
Peer collaboration	Almost always listens to, shares with, and supports the efforts of others in the group. Tries to keep people working well together.	Usually listens to, shares with, and supports the efforts of others in the group. Does not make waves in the group.	Often listens to, shares with, and supports the efforts of others in the group but sometimes is not a good team member.	Rarely listens to, shares with, and supports the efforts of others in the group. Often is not a good team member.
Physical	Stands up straight, looks relaxed and confident. Establishes eye contact.	Stands up straight and establishes eye contact.	Sometimes stands up straight and establishes eye contact.	Slouches or does not look at people during the presentation.

IMPROVISATIONAL ACTIVITY: ALPHABET

Lesson: Alphabet Book

Grade level: kindergarten

Subject: reading and language arts

Time length for lesson: this is a project that will take several class periods.

Lesson Overview In this lesson the students participate in the Alphabet improvisation game and create their own alphabet book in small groups.

Student Learning Objectives Students create physical representations of the alphabet, which aid the students in recognizing and creating the letters of the alphabet.

Instructional Plan and Explanation of Learning Activities

Step One: first class period: Teach the students the Alphabet game as described in Chapter Four. Let the students practice making letters in pairs.

Step Two: first class period: The teacher should take pictures of the students as they make letters, until all the letters of the alphabet are represented in the students' pairs.

Step Three: second class period: Prior to Step Three, the photos that were taken in the previous class should be developed. Give each student in the class a photo, which will be used to create an alphabet page. See the accompanying template (page 112) for the alphabet book pages.

Step Four: second class period: Once the students have created their alphabet page, the students and teacher bind the pages into a class book.

Assessment Plan for Lesson The students' work should be assessed for pictures that are included on the alphabet page, which includes pictures of items that begin with the same letter represented on the page. For example, the A page should have pictures of things such as apple, ant, alligator, or aardvark.

It's fun to learn how to physicalize letters.

| Place Photo of Students from the Class Here | Letter of the Alphabet Represented in Picture |
| | Words that represent the letter (i.e. A is for alligator, ant, apple |

Alphabet Book Template Page

Subject: Reading and Language Arts
Lesson: Alphabet Book

Grade Level	McREL Standards	Ontario Curriculum Ministry Expectations
Kindergarten	4. Gathers and uses information for research purposes 5. Uses the general skills and strategies of the reading process 8. Uses listening and speaking strategies for various purposes	8. Demonstrate a willingness to try new activities (e.g., experiment with new materials and tools, try out activities in a different learning center, join in the singing of a song, select and persist with challenging activities, experiment with writing) [C] 11. Interact cooperatively with others in classroom events and activities (e.g., offer and accept help in group situations, join in small- and large-group games and activities, join in democratic decision making) [C] 12. Adapt to new situations (e.g., having visitors in the classroom, having another teacher occasionally, going on a field trip, riding the school bus; initially, adapt with a great deal of support from the teachers; eventually, adapt with less assistance) [C] 13. Use a variety of simple strategies to solve social problems (e.g., seek assistance from the teacher when needed, use pictures or words to express their feelings, develop an awareness of honesty, talk to peers about possible solutions) [D]

IMPROVISATIONAL ACTIVITY: BEGINNING, MIDDLE, AND END

Lesson: Story Generation Using Beginning, Middle, and End

Grade level: third to sixth grade

Subject: English and language arts

Time length for lesson: forty-five to fifty minutes

Lesson Overview   Students generate ideas for creative writing as they play the improvisation game Beginning, Middle, End.

Student Learning Objectives   In this lesson, students review the elements of a short story and apply them to a written narrative of their own.

Instructional Plan and Explanation of Learning Activities

   Step One: If the students are unfamiliar with the improvisational game, teach them Beginning, Middle, End.

The teacher gives instructions for Beginning, Middle, and End.

Step Two: Once the students have completed a practice round of Beginning, Middle, End, the students should do another round.

Step Three: Once the students have completed several rounds of the improvisational game, as a large group discuss the possible topics and story ideas that were generated through the activity. Record the students' story ideas and topics on the chalkboard or on poster board so that they are visible to the entire classroom.

Step Four: Instruct the students to select one of the listed story ideas or topics and then write about it for twenty minutes.

Step Five: Give the students the opportunity to share with each other what they have drafted so far. The students can share their writing in pairs or as a large group through an "author's chair."

Step Six: Either in class or for homework, the students can revise their stories into final draft writing.

Assessment Plan for Lesson

This rubric can be used for the students' writing.

Subject: Reading and Language Arts Drama
Lesson: Story Generation Using Beginning, Middle, and End

Grade Level	McREL Standards	Ontario Curriculum Ministry Expectations
3 4 5 6	4. Gathers and uses information for research purposes 5. Uses the general skills and strategies of the reading process 8. Uses listening and speaking strategies for various purposes	**Reading** **Demonstrating understanding** **1.4** Demonstrate understanding of increasingly complex texts by summarizing and explaining important ideas and citing relevant supporting details **Making inferences, interpreting texts** **1.5** Develop interpretations about texts using stated and implied ideas to support their interpretations **Extending understanding** **1.6** Extend understanding of texts by connecting, comparing, and contrasting the ideas in them to their own knowledge, experience, and insights, to other familiar texts, and to the world around them **Interconnected skills** **4.2** Explain, in conversation with the teacher or peers or in a reader's notebook, how their skills in listening, speaking, writing, viewing, and representing help them make sense of what they read

Assessment Rubric for Beginning, Middle, End Short Story

Category	4	3	2	1
Creativity	The story contains many creative details that add to the audience's enjoyment. The author created an imaginative and interesting story.	The story contains a few creative details that add to the audience's enjoyment. The author has created and imaginative and interesting story.	The story contains a few creative details and descriptions, but they distract from the story. The author demonstrated effort in trying to create an imaginative and interesting story.	There is little evidence of creativity in the story. The author has not demonstrated effort in creating the story.
Beginning, Middle, and End	The beginning, middle, and end of the story are easy to understand and logical.	The beginning, middle, and end of the story are easy to understand and is somewhat logical.	The beginning, middle, and end of the story are sometimes difficult to follow and not always logical.	The beginning, middle, and end of the story are not attempted or are too difficult for the reader to follow.

IMPROVISATIONAL ACTIVITY: CONDUCTED STORY

Lesson: Conducting an American Revolution Review

Grade level: seventh to eighth grade

Subject: social studies

Time length for lesson: one class period of about forty-five to fifty minutes

Lesson Overview In this lesson, students use the improvisational game Conducted Story to discuss and analyze key events in the American Revolution.

Student Learning Objectives Students identify, review, and sequence key events in the American Revolution.

Instructional Plan and Explanation of Learning Activities

Step One: If the students are unfamiliar with the improvisational game Conducted Story, teach them the game and let each student participate at least one time.

Participating students cannot wait to get their turn
during Conducted Story.

Step Two: Distribute index cards and ask the students to write down a key event in the American Revolution. Here are some examples: Boston Tea Party, Boston Massacre, the Shot Heard Around the World, Paul Revere's ride, the Battle of Bunker Hill, First Continental Congress, and Thomas Jefferson writing the Declaration of Independence. Place all the cards in a hat.

Step Three: Six students should volunteer and stand in a performance line. Ask an audience member to select a card from the hat. The event is announced and the Conducted Story begins. The teacher directs the students who are participating in the Conducted Story. Before the performing students begin, ask the audience members to determine if there are any key facts missing from the story.

Continue with new students for each event. It is up to the students and teacher to determine when they have exhausted the events or the allotted time.

Assessment Plan for Lesson   There are several suggestions for assessing this activity:

- As a journal entry, ask the students to respond in writing: "What have you learned about the American Revolution in this activity, and why is it important?"

- Have the students draw a picture that graphically illustrates one of the American Revolution conducted stories they viewed in the class.

- In a large-group discussion or in small groups, ask the students to evaluate their own American Revolution conducted story.

  - "If you could redo your story, what would you do differently? Why?"

  - "What details did you include that were of historical importance? Why?"

  - "Think of an American Revolution event that was not presented that you would want to include next time. Why should this event be included?"

Subject: Social Studies
Lesson: Conducting an American Revolution Review

Grade Level	McREL Standards	Ontario Curriculum Ministry Expectations
7 8	6. Understands the causes of the American Revolution, the ideas and interests involved in shaping the revolutionary movement, and reasons for the American victory 7. Understands the impact of the American Revolution on politics and economy	By the end of grade 7, students will: • Explain the origins of English settlement in British North America after the fall of New France; describe the migration and settlement experiences of the various groups of settlers; and outline the causes, events, and results of the War of 1812 • Use a variety of resources and tools to gather, process, and communicate information about the beginnings and development of the new British colonies

IMPROVISATIONAL ACTIVITY: CREATING A SONG

Lesson: Speaking in Songs

Grade level: seventh to eighth grade

Subject: visual arts

Time length for lesson: broken into three parts, total instructional time is eighty minutes.

Huda Siksek from Ontario, Canada, created this lesson.

Lesson Overview　　Using improvisation exercises, the students learn about key visual artists and demonstrate what they have learned through cooperatively created songs that employ improvisational activities.

Learning Objectives　　Students learn to:

- Work well with others, supporting their team for a common goal
- Memorize and interpret lesson content through creative improvisation
- Develop creative solutions for song ideas
- Become empowered with voice and confidence
- Present in front of the class without fear (for first-timers)
- Work with a team, distributing and sharing tasks and becoming involved
- Experience friendly competition
- Channel physical energy into a lesson (away from desks)
- Monitor and analyze their own behavior and others'
- Develop awareness of group dynamics and how their energy affects others as well as the general outcome of the activity

Students will be planning, thinking, responding, creating, performing, connecting, observing (as audience), imagining, participating, contributing, communicating, engaging, and learning while they play.

This lesson works with any subject and almost any topic. For visual arts, this exercise works best for an art history lesson content (for example: impressionism, African ritual masks, Frida Kahlo, medieval art, Inuit art, or any data that are factual or have certain characteristics, such as the characteristics of Henry Moore's sculptures or Persian carpets).

Students listen eagerly to their classmates.

This activity also works best as the third part of an art history lesson but is flexible for the teacher. This is how I successfully led this exercise.

Part One (forty minutes): Teacher delivers factual information to the students, such as a lesson handout, slide show, or film about the general topic to ensure that all students have the same information on the topic.

Part Two (forty minutes): Students make a creative fact page or artist profile in their sketchbooks to include main points, biographical information, and some sketches or pictures. They must include fifteen to twenty notes from the handout from the previous lesson, as well as design, decorate, and use color in their sketchbook pages (a two-page spread).

Part Three (eighty minutes): Speaking in Songs activity: Students learn how to work as team members to write and perform a song about the unit topic. In small groups, they review the previous class handouts, write songs, and then present the songs during the last part of the lesson. Finally, students fill out a feedback form (rubric).

Instructional Plan and Explanation of Learning Activities

Step One: Warm-up activity. Write "Lesson today: Speaking in Songs" on the board in big letters. When students enter the classroom, they will ask what it means. Answer them in song (to the tune of "Happy Birthday"): "Today you will sing / about Indian art." If you model the behavior, this breaks the ice and pulls them in. They will start responding with song. If you prefer not to sing, just explain verbally.

Step Two: Divide class into groups of five. Students should not pick their friends. Random selection according to any selection activity (such as tribes activity,* or picking numbers from a basket, or drawing five each of stars, moons, suns, and hearts and letting students pick without looking to make four designated groups, as with all the stars together). Make sure you check attendance before you do this and have the correct number of pictures or numbers in the basket.

Step Three: Announce the activity: "Today you will be talking in songs. You and your team will present the Impressionism lesson (or Frida Kahlo, or another topic) to the class through a song."

Step Four: Announce the rules:

- Every team will present a song at the end of class today.

- The song should be about one minute long (five to ten lines in the song).

- You may use your handout from last lesson or notes on this topic.

- When you present your song, your team will stand at the front of the class. You must present to the whole class, not only to the teacher. So be sure you make eye contact with everyone around the room. Be sure every member of your team is seen.

- During presentations, while your team is not presenting, sit and listen respectfully to the other songs. You must show respect, support, and encouragement. Do not interrupt.

---

*Tribes activity: Teacher will pick teams as follows. Line up the whole class in one single file, and ask the students to sort themselves according to birth date, with one end being January and the other December. Once lined up, count the first five as a team, and continue until they all have a team. Ask students to return to corners of room or stations, and sit with their team. They can even sit on the floor or on top of desks.

- Every member of your team must participate (even if only saying one word). You must show that you are working well together, letting everyone have input, not taking over and not offending or insulting anyone. Speak to your team members using positive language. Let everyone speak before you make decisions. Learn and understand how teamwork happens when everyone helps to reach a shared goal.

- You may use any song; make it up or change the lyrics to an existing song such as "Happy Birthday" or "Jingle Bells."

- Any questions? Anything else we should talk about? (Here they will ask you if they can use swear words. Guide them to use appropriate language because this is a professional learning environment where visitors might walk by and all students need to behave and speak using appropriate language that reflects positively on them, the school, and everyone involved. They will also ask you if they can add dance steps or props; sure!)

Step Five: Distribute the rubric and read along with them. Tell them they must fill it out later, before the end of class. Ask volunteers to read it out loud. Answer questions if they have any.

Step Six: Start the Speaking in Songs activity: "You have thirty-five minutes starting now. You may go with your team to any area in the room to work on your song. We will do the presentations at 3:15." (Give them ten-minute and five-minute warnings before the end.)

While students prepare their songs around the room, you should walk around and listen respectfully and encouragingly. Do not correct or change what the students are creating. Let them have fun and be creative. This activity is not about content, but it is about students attempting to create a song with others within a time limit, and about building public speaking confidence.

Step Seven: After thirty minutes or so, announce: "OK, presentations in one minute; which team wants to go first?"

The teacher must give a couple of minutes for each group to present at the end, so if there are four groups then start about fifteen minutes before the end of class. All groups must present their song at the end of class. Make sure you initiate clapping and cheering for each group. If you run out of time, keep them over. If you send them home without hearing their song and tell them they will present next class, they will leave feeling disappointed, and by next class the momentum will be gone. It is important to plan the presentation time so that every team presents its song.

During the presentations, the teacher should sit at the back of the room and let students enjoy one another's songs. No judgment or evaluation of their songs. Watch out for put-downs or jeering, but if you did the rubric with them before the activity then this should not happen.

As for the rubric, in my experience there is so much excitement at the end (or we run out of time) that they rarely have time to complete them properly. The value for me is to go over the rubric with them before the activity so they can absorb some of the "descriptors" which are really expectations of behavior. See self-evaluation for this lesson (page 127).

Try these:

- Vote for best song (prize could be that the winning team gets to leave first).

- Perform the songs to a third grade class (or any younger class).

- Perform the songs at the annual art exhibition if they are good.

- Teams come up with band names for their team and titles for their songs.

- Next class: students write a short reflection in their sketchbooks about the experience (and illustrate it). They must use color even for the writing part. Scan and print these pages and put them up on a bulletin board.

- Structure the songs if you have a long lesson or if you want to extend this to a double lesson (for example, add a chorus and two verses to the song).

- Link to performance art and make the song their artistic final product.

- As a review for the final exam, do a "Canadian Idol" concert in class, with each team singing one unit, so they are doing different topics. The second or third time you do this activity, allow students to do solos, or work in pairs if they request it, keeping an eye on the others so no one gets left out.

- Play a karaoke tape (music only, no lyrics) of a sampling of famous songs, and ask the teams to all use the same song as their melody. See how they all come up with different lyrics.

Assessment Plan for Lesson   See (page 127).

Additional Comments from Huda Siksek   I found that filming the songs puts some students under pressure, which takes away from the experience. Instead, once I asked them to repeat their performance a second time, so that I could video it, and they accepted the idea enthusiastically and asked me to e-mail them copies of the tape. Some of them feel anxious if they see the video camera on my desk at the start of the lesson.

This lesson plan was invented during class as a suggestion from one of my students who asked if we could do "Whose line is it anyway?" in class instead of a final exam. He particularly liked the "hoe down" songs at the end, so that's how this activity was born. I am a huge fan of comedy and improv, so it was easy for me to say yes to this type of activity. I have space in the art room for it.

My most rewarding experience with this lesson was seeing the shy students who don't usually participate or contribute stand up and sing with the team, with big smiles on their faces because they're having fun and engaging with each other without fear.

Great reward: seeing the rowdy, energetic students channel their energy into performance with the whole class as their audience, so they are not distracting anyone.

Subject: Visual Art Lesson: Speaking in Songs		
Grade Level	McREL Standards	Ontario Curriculum Ministry Expectations
7 8	3. Knows a range of subject matter, symbols, and potential ideas in the visual arts 4. Understands the visual arts in relation to history and cultures	• Students will identify the principles of design (emphasis, rhythm, balance, unity, variety, proportion) and use them in ways appropriate for this grade in producing and responding to works of art • Students will correctly use vocabulary and art terminology associated with the specific expectations for this grade • Students will define the principles of design (emphasis, balance, rhythm, unity, variety, proportion) and use them in ways appropriate for this grade in producing and responding to works of art • Students will correctly use vocabulary and art terminology associated with the specific expectations for this grade

Self-Evaluation
Speaking in Songs

Individual Self-Evaluation

I felt comfortable working with my team. (Select as many as you like.)

- ❑ Yes, they were all great!
- ❑ We worked together to meet our goal.
- ❑ No, some of them were not acting in an appropriate way.
- ❑ Most of the time things were flowing smoothly.
- ❑ I'd work with them again.
- ❑ I showed my team respect, support, and encouragement.
- ❑ I showed the other teams respect, support, and encouragement.

My best contribution to my team today was:

_____

_____

_____

I looked around and noticed this behavior was happening:

_____

_____

_____

Feedback for the teacher to make this activity better next year:

_____

_____

_____

_____

I participated in the following ways: (select as many as you like)

- ❑ I spoke frequently, but I also listened attentively to my teammates.
- ❑ I spoke all the time, and I don't remember what anyone else said.

- ❑ I let others talk, and I welcomed their contributions.
- ❑ I interrupted the others, or yelled a lot, or acted rowdy.
- ❑ I was interrupted frequently by others.
- ❑ I contributed in a wonderful way to the song.
- ❑ I had no input at all to the song.
- ❑ I really enjoyed the presentation and singing part the most.
- ❑ I really enjoyed inventing the song and preparing it the most.
- ❑ It was all fun because

_____

- ❑ It was not all fun because

_____

If I had to mark my team song, I would give it _____ out of 10 because

_____

_____

_____

Group Evaluation of Another Team's Song

The best song in my opinion was

_____ because

_____

_____

_____

I admired the way some students presented their songs; if I could do it all over again, I would do some things differently, for example:

_____

_____

_____

_____

IMPROVISATIONAL ACTIVITY: DR. KNOW-IT-ALL

Lesson: Becoming Characters

Grade level: fifth to eighth grade

Subject: language arts

Time length for lesson: one class period of about forty-five to fifty minutes

Lesson Overview   In this lesson, the students apply the improvisational game Dr. Know-It-All to a character review.

Student Learning Objectives   The students use oral language to analyze and review characterization.

Instructional Plan and Explanation of Learning Activities   To aid in the exploration of this lesson, *To Kill a Mockingbird* is the referenced text.

Step One: If the students are unfamiliar with the improvisational game Dr. Know-It-All, teach it to them by following the directions from the previous chapter.

Step Two: Prior to this exercise, review the main characters of the novel:

Jean Louise "Scout" Finch

Jeremy Atticus "Jem" Finch

Atticus Finch

Arthur "Boo" Radley

Tom Robinson

Robert E. Lee "Bob" Ewell

Mayella Violet Ewell

Step Three: Six students volunteer and create a performance line. Ask a student audience member to select a character. Before the students ask questions of the Dr.-Know-It-All student performers, ask the student audience to write down questions for the character. For example, say that Dr. Know-It-All is Scout. The students then create questions they would like to ask this character, such as:

"Why weren't you afraid of Boo Radley when you met him for the first time?"

"What do you like most about your brother, Jem?"

Play several rounds of the game.

Assessment Plan for Lesson   Once the students have completed their questioning, ask them to write a literature letter to one of the characters. Literature letters are personal expressions that readers create in letter form about novels and stories. The letters are addressed to peers, teachers, or other interested parties, who may or may not have read the literature in question.

Subject: Language Arts
Lesson: Becoming Characters

Grade Level	McREL Standards	Ontario Curriculum Ministry Expectations
5 6 7 8	4. Gathers and uses information for research purposes 5. Uses the general skills and strategies of the reading process 8. Uses listening and speaking strategies for various purposes	**Reading** **Demonstrating understanding** **1.4** Demonstrate understanding of increasingly complex texts by summarizing and explaining important ideas and citing relevant supporting details **Making inferences, interpreting texts** **1.5** Develop interpretations about texts using stated and implied ideas to support their interpretations **Extending understanding** **1.6** Extend understanding of texts by connecting, comparing, and contrasting the ideas in them to their own knowledge, experience, and insights, to other familiar texts, and to the world around them **Interconnected skills** **4.2** Explain, in conversation with the teacher or peers or in a reader's notebook, how their skills in listening, speaking, writing, viewing, and representing help them make sense of what they read

IMPROVISATIONAL ACTIVITY: GIBBERISH TRANSLATOR

Lesson: Math Gibberish Translator

Grade level: fifth to eighth grade
Subject: mathematics
Time length for lesson: twenty to thirty minutes

Lesson Overview   This lesson was created by Bradley Berlage, a mathematics and English teacher in Chicago. This activity can enhance students' understanding of mathematical concepts and how to apply them.

Student Learning Objectives   The students discuss mathematical concepts accurately and build a sense of self-efficacy with these mathematical concepts.

Instructional Plan and Explanation of Learning Activities

Step One: Students will be introduced to the Gibberish Translator activity, usually first encountered during a previous class period.

Step Two: The teacher prepares a list of mathematical concepts to use in the Math Gibberish Translator exercise and writes them on the board. As students become more familiar with the improvisation exercise, they can come up with their own examples. Some ideas that you may want to use:

- Two cavemen talking about which shape would work best to make a wheel

- Two brothers or sisters fighting about who did better in a video game (using percentages)

- Two toy company salespeople debating which type of graph best depicts the sales of the newest toy

Step Three: Play four rounds of the game.

Assessment Plan for Lesson   Have the students respond to these questions, either in a group or on paper in their math journals:

- Did you feel the translator was doing an accurate job of translating? Why or why not?

- Did you feel that the translator provided an accurate use of (the mathematical concept)? If no, what was missing?

- What should we translate next time? (Be sure to include a mathematical concept that we are currently covering.)

Subject: Mathematics Lesson: Math Gibberish Translator		
Grade Level	**McREL Standards**	**Ontario Curriculum Ministry Expectations**
5 6 7 8	**1.** Uses a variety of strategies in the problem-solving process **9.** Understands the general nature and uses of mathematics	• **Reasoning and Proving** Students will apply developing reasoning skills (e.g., pattern recognition, classification) to make and investigate conjectures. • **Reflecting** Students will demonstrate that they are reflecting on and monitoring their thinking to help clarify their understanding as they complete an investigation or solve a problem. • **Connecting** Students will make connections among mathematical concepts and procedures, and relate mathematical ideas to situations or phenomena drawn from other contexts. • **Communicating** Students will communicate mathematical thinking orally, visually, and in writing, using everyday language, a basic mathematical vocabulary, and a variety of representations as well as observe basic mathematical conventions.

IMPROVISATIONAL ACTIVITY: GIVE AND TAKE

Lesson: Building a Relationship

Grade level: first to fifth grade

Subject: all content areas. This lesson is designed to build classroom community.

Time length for lesson: forty-five minutes

Liz Hamilton, a teacher from Staten Island, New York, created this lesson.

Lesson Overview   Each student learns how to work as an ensemble through a few exercises involving thinking *outside the box*. The objective is to build trust between the students and trust within themselves. It is important to encourage students at this age to use their imaginations. This lesson gives each student the chance to find his or her voice and place within a large group. Students build self-esteem not only through their creative performance but through their contribution to the class.

Students learn about the important principle of Give and Take, which is essential for all improvisation games.

Student Learning Objectives Students learn the importance of ensemble, how to work as a team, and how to trust themselves and each other. These young performers discover that they can multitask onstage and in the classroom. Giving a student an objective that is three-dimensional is much more challenging than a singular objective. The exercises explained here give the performer the opportunity to learn how to cope with a number of priorities.

Instructional Plan and Explanation of Learning Activities

Step One: It is critical for children to feel safe in their environment. The nature of improvisational work might be different from their everyday classroom routine. It is the teacher's goal to have your students feel safe. To do this, you must break the barriers between your future performers. The students learn about the Second City foundational concept of Give and Take through these activities.

Name Spring is one exercise a teacher can use for students to remember their classmates' names. The game involves tossing a beanbag around a circle and shouting the name of the classmate to whom the beanbag is being thrown. Performers juggle priorities while onstage; this initial game involves acting and reacting, memorization, and voice projection.

Body awareness and expression are vital to a performer. Young artists tend to be less inhibited and more comfortable with their bodies. This development should be facilitated at a young age.

Step Two: The game Alphabet Soup gives players a chance to work in groups of five or six in creating letters of the alphabet as the teacher calls out each letter. This exercise teaches students how to create and communicate within a team atmosphere. It also gives performers a chance to use their body as a performance tool—something they will need down the line for character work.

Step Three: The final game of today's lesson is One-Word Story. The young performers sit in a large circle and are given the opportunity to contribute one word to the story created among the group. The story continues around the group a few times before more variables are added to the exercise. You, the instructor, will ask them to sit shoulder to shoulder now and have them continue with a new story. This story should be more fluid, without any gaps. Once students understand this concept, they will stop thinking and just react. They make their own discoveries instead of being told what to do. This freedom among young performers is not only a useful tool but liberating to their imagination.

Assessment Plan for Lesson The teacher should observe the students and determine how they are working together as an ensemble.

Subject: All Content Areas
Lesson: Building a Relationship

Grade Level	McREL Standards	Ontario Curriculum Ministry Expectations
Kindergarten 1 2 3 4 5	**Working with others: standards** 1. Contributes to the overall effort of a group 2. Uses conflict-resolution techniques 3. Works well with diverse individuals and in diverse situations 4. Displays effective interpersonal communication skills 5. Demonstrates leadership skills **Thinking and reasoning: standards** 1. Understands and applies the basic principles of presenting an argument 2. Understands and applies basic principles of logic and reasoning 3. Effectively uses mental processes that are based on identifying similarities and differences 4. Understands and applies basic principles of hypothesis testing and scientific inquiry 5. Applies basic troubleshooting and problem-solving techniques 6. Applies decision-making techniques	8. Demonstrate a willingness to try new activities 11. Interact cooperatively with others in classroom events and activities 12. Adapt to new situations 13. Use a variety of simple strategies to solve social problems

IMPROVISATIONAL ACTIVITY: OBJECT WORK

Lesson: Geometric Object Work

Grade level: fourth to eighth grade

Subject: mathematics, geometric shapes

Time length for lesson: ten to fifteen minutes

This lesson was created by Bradley Berlage, a mathematics and English teacher in Chicago.

Lesson Overview   This kinesthetic activity can be used to give students a real-world application of geometric shapes and figures.

Student Learning Objectives   The students identify geometric figures in the real world.

Instructional Plan and Explanation of Learning Activities

Step One: Students are introduced to the Object Work activity, usually first encountered during a previous class period.

Step Two: Teacher prepares a list of figures and geometric terms that he or she wants the students to become familiar with. These terms and pictures of these figures are also placed on the walls around the classroom. They might include:

Circle

Triangle

Square

Point

Line

Cube

Sphere

Cone

Pyramid

Octagon

Rectangle

Step Three: The teacher reminds the students of the Object Work exercise they did previously and introduces the Geometric Object Work exercise with a simple example that she starts. The teacher starts the exercise and then passes the object to another person. This continues until all students who want to participate have had a chance to create an object.

This student's concentration is evident in her Object Work.

Step Four: At the end of the exercise, the teacher has each student review the object they created. While she is doing that, the students write down the geometric shape *and* the object that was created with that shape.

Step Five: After all students have written down the object and the shape, the teacher has each student announce the object and shape that he or she made.

Assessment Plan for Lesson   After the exercise, the students respond to these questions in their notebooks:

- How are geometric shapes used in real life?
- How has your opinion about shapes changed?
- Did you learn something new about geometric shapes?
- What did you like about this exercise? What did you not like?

Subject: Mathematics
Lesson: Geometric Object Work

Grade Level	McREL Standards	Ontario Curriculum Ministry Expectations
1	1. Uses a variety of strategies in the problem-solving process 5. Understands and applies basic and advanced properties of the concepts of geometry 9. Understands the general nature and uses of mathematics	• **Reflecting** Students will demonstrate that they are reflecting on and monitoring their thinking to help clarify their understanding as they complete an investigation or solve a problem. • **Connecting** Students will make connections among mathematical concepts and procedures, and relate mathematical ideas to situations or phenomena drawn from other contexts. • **Representing** Students will create basic representations of simple mathematical ideas. • **Communicating** Students will communicate mathematical thinking orally, visually, and in writing, using everyday language, a basic mathematical vocabulary, and a variety of representations as well as observe basic mathematical conventions.

IMPROVISATIONAL ACTIVITY: ONE-WORD STORY

Lesson: One-Word Story, a Many-Word Story

Grade level: second to eighth grade

Subject: language arts

Time length for lesson: one class period of about forty-five to fifty minutes

Lesson Overview   Using the improvisational game One-Word Story, as a pre-writing activity the students create a short story.

Student Learning Objectives   The students participate in the writing process in order to create a short story.

Instructional Plan and Explanation of Learning Activities

Step One: If the students do not already know the improvisation game One-Word Story, teach the game according to the directions given in Chapter Four.

Students are ready to participate in One-Word Story.

Step Two: The students should participate in the game for several rounds. The teacher should keep a record of the stories that are told as a result of the game.

Step Three: Once the students have participated in several rounds of the game, instruct them to create a short story using one of the one-word stories that were created in class.

Assessment Plan for Lesson   The rubric on page 141 can be used to evaluate the students' stories.

Subject: Language Arts
Lesson: One Word Story, a Many Word Story

Grade Level	McREL Standards	Ontario Curriculum Ministry Expectations
2 3 4 5 6 7 8	4. Gathers and uses information for research purposes 5. Uses the general skills and strategies of the reading process 8. Uses listening and speaking strategies for different purposes	**Demonstrating understanding** **1.4** Demonstrate understanding of increasingly complex texts by summarizing and explaining important ideas and citing relevant supporting details **Making inferences, interpreting texts** **1.5** develop interpretations about texts using stated and implied ideas to support their interpretations **Extending understanding** **1.6** Extend understanding of texts by connecting, comparing, and contrasting the ideas in them to their own knowledge, experience, and insights, to other familiar texts, and to the world around them **Interconnected skills** **4.2** Explain, in conversation with the teacher and/or peers or in a reader's notebook, how their skills in listening, speaking, writing, viewing, and representing help them make sense of what they read

Story Writing: One Word into Many Words

Category	4	3	2	1
Writing Process	Student follows the writing process (prewriting, drafting, reviewing, and editing) to create an enjoyable story.	Student follows the writing process (prewriting, drafting, reviewing, and editing) to create a structured story.	Student generally follows the writing process (prewriting, drafting, reviewing, and editing) to create a good story.	Student does not follow the writing process (prewriting, drafting, reviewing, and editing) and the story is difficult to follow.
Organization	The story is well organized and logical.	The story is generally well organized. There may be scenes that do not follow logically.	The story is organized but difficult to follow at times.	The scenes and story events do not follow logically. The story is difficult to follow.
Creativity	The story contains many creative details that add to the audience's enjoyment. The author created an imaginative and interesting story.	The story contains a few creative details that add to the audience's enjoyment. The author has created and imaginative and interesting story.	The story contains a few creative details and descriptions, but they distract from the story. The author demonstrated effort in trying to create an imaginative and interesting story.	There is little evidence of creativity in the story. The author has not demonstrated effort in creating the story.
Setting	Vivid words and descriptions are used to clearly establish the setting.	Some vivid words and descriptions are used to clearly establish the setting.	Although the author does not apply a lot of detail, the reader can figure out the setting of the story.	It is difficult for the reader to figure out the setting of the story because of the lack of detail that is provided by the writer.

IMPROVISATIONAL ACTIVITY: PARTS OF A WHOLE

Lesson: Physicalizing Cell Structure

Grade level: fourth to eighth grade
Subject: biology
Time length for lesson: thirty minutes

Lesson Overview   In this lesson, the students use the improvisational game Parts of a Whole to physicalize and create cells, the building blocks of life.

Student Learning Objectives   Students review and physicalize cell structure.

Instructional Plan and Explanation of Learning Activities

Step One: If the students are unfamiliar with Parts of a Whole, teach the students the game and give them the opportunity to play it.

Step Two: Review cell structure with the students. Here are Web sites that have templates and information about cell structure for kids:

- http://www.cellsalive.com/ Cells Alive is a Web site that contains many pictures about cells and of mitosis and meiosis.
- http://www.biology4kids.com/ Offers copious resources on cell structure and function.
- http://www.brainpop.com/science/livingsystems/cellstructures/ This site offers an animated version of cell structure and function.

Step Three: The students should be divided into groups of about five. Each group presents a physical representation of a cell using the Parts of a Whole exercise. As each student physicalizes the cell part, remind him or her to call it out ("I am the cell wall" or "I am the nucleolus!").

Step Four: Once the students have created their cell representations through the improvisation game, they can expand the activity to include cell division. The students can recreate mitosis and meiosis.

Assessment Plan for Lesson   Let the students create their cells in the activity without formal assessment. The teacher can observe and offer sidecoaching if the students are presenting incorrect information. But remember: the activity teaches the students the content, and they need the space to experiment. As an informal assessment, ask the students to create a plant cell or an animal cell. Once the students create the appointed cell, see how many parts were included and ask the students in the audience for any parts that might be missing. For a more formal assessment, give the students a blank cell part handout to determine how much they have learned about cell structure.

Subject: Science		
Lesson: Physicalizing Cell Structure		

Grade Level	McREL Standards	Ontario Curriculum Ministry Expectations
4	5. Understands the structure and function of cells and organisms 6. Understands relationships among organisms and their physical environment 11. Understands the nature of scientific knowledge 12. Understands the nature of scientific inquiry	• Demonstrate an understanding of the concepts of habitat and community, and identify the factors that could affect habitats and communities of plants and animals
5		• Identify the cell as the basic unit of life
6		• Describe microscopic living things using appropriate tools to assist them with their observations (e.g., nets and microscopes for pond study)
7		• Use appropriate vocabulary, including correct science and technology terminology, to communicate ideas, procedures, and results (e.g., use scientific terms such as *biosphere, biome, ecosystem, species*)
8		• Identify unicellular organisms (e.g., amoebae) and multicellular organisms (e.g., worms, humans); recognize that cells in multicellular organisms investigate ways in which unicellular organisms meet their basic needs (e.g., for food, movement) • Need to reproduce to make more cells to form and repair tissues

IMPROVISATIONAL ACTIVITY: SLIDE SHOW

Lesson: "Ten Days in a Madhouse" Human Slide Show

Grade level: eighth grade

Subject: English and American history

Time length for lesson: three fifty-minute class periods

Rose Ryan, national board certified teacher from Schaumburg, Illinois, created this three-class-period lesson.

Lesson Overview Students read and understand how Nellie Bly's "Ten Days in a Madhouse" applies to the muckraking era of American history and literature.

In groups of four or five, students are assigned a chapter from Bly's "Ten Days in a Madhouse"; after reading its assigned chapter, the group creates two still "human slide show" slides that represent the events of the assigned chapter.

Once all groups have prepared their slides, each group performs its slides in person in the order in which the chapters occur in the Bly piece. The ultimate goal is the students' creation of a "Ten Days in a Madhouse" human slide show.

Student Learning Objectives Students will:

- Read and understand "Ten Days in a Madhouse," including how it fits into the muckraking genre (biased journalism for social justice), plot, character, historical context, and theme.

- Make connections between the text and their lives or prior knowledge.

- Use specific textual evidence to answer the questions posed in their small groups.

- Listen and respond to their peers' ideas during their discussion.

- Create two physical slides that demonstrate their understanding of their chapter, to be presented to the class in the order in which chapters occur in Bly's work.

Instructional Plan and Explanation of Learning Activities Before the lesson, historical context of muckraking era will already have been taught.

Because this lesson spans three class periods, the instructional plans is divided into three class periods.

Students are attentive listeners as they receive directions
from their teacher for Slide Show.

Period One

- Introduce the lesson; give students a handout and character list (see page 148).
- Allow students to choose groups, and assign those groups chapters from "Ten Days in a Madhouse."
- Students read assigned chapter with their group.
- *Homework*: Finish reading chapter and bring ideas for slides tomorrow.

Period Two

- Students work in groups to coordinate slides, making sure that all group members are involved in preparing two physical slides.
- *Homework*: Bring any props and costumes needed for slide show tomorrow.

Period Three

- Give groups five minutes to prepare for the slide show.
- Students perform slide show for whole class.

Assessment Plan for Lesson   Students are assessed by the teacher on (1) the presentation of their final two slides and (2) the narrator's justification or explanation of each slide. They also assess their fellow group members' contributions in confidential group evaluations.

Additional Comments and Tips from the Teacher   I used this lesson plan in my National Board certification process (the only way to become a "master teacher" in the state of Illinois), and the board reviewers were complimentary of the activity, the sophistication of students' interpretations, and the creativity of the idea. It was my highest instructional score in my portfolio, and it helped me achieve National Board status in November 2005.

Subject: Language Arts and American History
Lesson: "Ten Days in a Madhouse" Human Slide Show

Grade Level	McREL Standards	Ontario Curriculum Ministry Expectations
8 (language arts)	1. Uses the general skills and strategies of the writing process 5. Uses the general skills and strategies of the reading process 6. Uses reading skills and strategies to understand and interpret a variety of literary texts 8. Uses listening and speaking strategies for different purposes	**Understanding media text:** **Purpose and audience** **1.1** Explain how a variety of media texts address their intended purpose and audience (e.g., this stage production based on a popular novel uses music and lighting to enhance the original and appeal to its fans; this commercial for a sports car uses fast-paced editing and rock music to appeal to the target audience of young, single men and women)

Grade Level	McREL Standards	Ontario Curriculum Ministry Expectations
	10. Understands the characteristics and components of the media	**Production perspectives** **1.6** Identify who produces various media texts and determine the commercial, ideological, political, cultural, or artistic interests or perspectives that the texts may involve (e.g., a music company's interest in a recording may be different from that of the artist; the company that produces a video game and the game's creator may have differing views on how the game should be promoted) **Conventions and techniques** **2.2** Identify the conventions and techniques used in a variety of media forms and explain how they help convey meaning and influence or engage the audience (e.g., Website conventions: home pages provide users with a convenient preview of the types of information available; Website techniques: "sidebars" with inviting audio and video elements entice viewers to browse and explore new topics that might not have been their first priority)
8 (American history)	20. Understands how Progressives and others addressed problems of industrial capitalism, urbanization, and political corruption	

Human Slide Show:
"Ten Days in a Madhouse" by Nellie Bly

BASIC PREMISE

In 1887, journalist Nellie Bly began an investigative journey to Blackwell's Island, an "insane asylum" for women, as an undercover report for the *New York World*. Bly had to find someone to commit her to the asylum first and then fool a team of doctors into thinking she was insane. Once committed to the asylum, Bly continued to pose as a patient for ten days until the *World* removed her from the asylum.

CHAPTERS EXAMINED

VIII	Inside the Madhouse
IX	An Expert (?) at Work
X	My First Supper
XI	In the Bath
XI, 2	In the Bath, cont.
XII	Promenading with Lunatics
XIII	Choking and Beating Patients
XIV	Some Unfortunate Stories
XIV, 2	Some Unfortunate Stories, cont.
XV	Incidents of Asylum Life
XVI	The Last Good-bye
XVII	The Grand Jury Investigation

All text copied from http://digital.library.upenn.edu/women/bly/madhouse/madhouse.html.

YOUR GROUP'S TASK

Each group will put together a piece of the "Ten Days in a Madhouse" slide show our class is creating.

The group's essential question is, "How does your chapter fit into Bly's piece?"

First, your group will read its assigned chapter. Then your group will discuss the answers to the discussion questions listed below. Make sure to record your answers!

Finally, your group will present two live slides that capture the essence of your chapter.

QUESTIONS

What is the biggest discovery Bly makes in this chapter?

How does her physical environment affect Bly?

How did the hospital and asylum staff get away with their cruel actions?

How is your chapter of "Ten Days in a Madhouse" a good example of realism?

SLIDE SHOW

With your group, you will create a living slide show that adds to our class's understanding of "Ten Days in a Madhouse."

You will present two live slides. "Live" means members of your group pose in the front of the room.

All group members must participate.

Each group will need a narrator for the two slides. The narrator's job is to explain what's going on in each slide.

Slides should be insightful and creative. The two slides should be noticeably different.

Today: Read your chapter, answer the discussion questions, and plan your slides.

Tomorrow: Present slides to class during second hour.

CHARACTERS TO KNOW

Some characters reoccur throughout Bly's piece. Because you have only one chapter, the names referenced by Bly will not be familiar to you. Use these character descriptions to enhance your understanding of your chapter.

Nellie Brown/Nellie Moreno—Bly's pseudonyms used during her investigation

Mrs. Stanard—the matron of a house for runaway girls

Judge Duffy—kindly judge to whom girls are brought for insanity questioning

Policeman Brockert—guard in charge of transporting possibly insane girls

Mary—nurse at the hospital where Bly awaits being found insane; bribes girls for money

(continued)

Miss Scott—matron of the hospital where girls are taken for physical insanity testing

Dr. Field—doctor examining girls in hospital for insanity

Miss Tillie Maynard—patient committed with Bly

Miss Annie Neville—patient committed with Bly

Mrs. Fox—patient committed with Bly

Mrs. Louise Schanz—patient committed with Bly

Warden O'Rourke—security guard of hospital where Bly awaits being found insane

Miss Grupe—nurse at insane asylum

Dr. Kinier—doctor at insane asylum

Miss McCarten—nurse at insane asylum

Dr. Ingram—doctor who spoke to Bly while she was in the asylum

Miss Grady—head nurse of asylum

Superintendent Dent—in charge of the asylum; very distant from the patients

Louise—asylum patient, said to have fever of 150 degrees

Urena Little-Page—patient at asylum who lies about age and is abused by nurses

Mrs. Grady/Mrs. O'Keefe—older asylum patient beaten by nurses

Matilda—asylum patient abused by nurses

Josephine Despreau—French woman patient choked by asylum nurses

Sarah Fishbaum—Hebrew woman patient committed by her husband

Mrs. McCartney—asylum patient

Mary Hughes—asylum patient

Carrie Glass—"idiot" asylum patient, according to Bly

Margaret—asylum patient committed for cleaning kitchen floor

Mrs. Turney—asylum patient put on "rope gang" for acting out against a nurse

Mrs. Cotter—woman abused by nurses for thinking her husband was coming up sidewalk

Miss Hart, Mrs. Kroener, Miss Fitzpatrick, Miss Finney, Miss Conway—asylum nurses

Miss Mattie Morgan—asylum patient who plays music for visitors

Pauline Moser—asylum patient

IMPROVISATIONAL ACTIVITY: SPACE WALK

Lesson: Geometry Walk

Grade level: fourth to eighth grade

Subject: mathematics, geometry

Time length for lesson: ten to fifteen minutes

This lesson was created by Bradley Berlage, a mathematics and English teacher in Chicago.

Lesson Overview Through movement, the students will experience and explore geometry shapes. Through kinesthetic representation, the students will internalize the characteristics of specific geometric forms.

Student Learning Objectives The students develop a personal connection with geometric figures through kinesthetic movement.

Instructional Plan and Explanation of Learning Activities

Step One: Teacher prepares a list of figures and geometric terms that he or she wants the students to become familiar with. These terms and pictures of these figures are also placed on the walls around the classroom. They might include:

Acute angles

Obtuse angles

Circle

Triangle

Square

Point

Line

Cube

Sphere

Cone

Step Two: Students are introduced to the Space Walk activity, usually first encountered during a previous class period.

Step Three: For the Geometry Walk, the students are reminded about the Space Walk and now participate during the geometry walk.

Students explore their environment during Space Walk.

Step Four: After the walk, the students participate in a class discussion. Students write their responses on poster paper, responding to these questions:

- How did you feel when you were moving through the space as (an acute angle, circle, cube, and so on)?
- What did you notice about other people?
- Which walk took up more space?
- Which walk was more difficult?
- If you were to make an object that moved, which geometric figure would you probably want to use to move?
- Which one would you not want to use?
- Which one of the geometric figures could hold a lot?
- Which geometric figure could hold the least?

Step Five: Students are each asked to write a response to the prompt: "From doing the geometry walk, I learned. . . ."

Assessment Plan for Lesson To determine the students' growing understanding of the concepts, they are evaluated on the basis of their written responses and their active participation in the exercise.

<table>
<tr><td colspan="3" align="center">**Subject: Mathematics**
Lesson: Geometry Walk</td></tr>
<tr><td>**Grade
Level**</td><td>**McREL Standards**</td><td>**Ontario Curriculum Ministry Expectations**</td></tr>
<tr>
<td></td>
<td>1. Uses a variety of strategies in the problem-solving process

5. Understands and applies basic and advanced properties of the concepts of geometry

9. Understands the general nature and uses of mathematics</td>
<td>• **Reflecting** Students will demonstrate that they are reflecting on and monitoring their thinking to help clarify their understanding as they complete an investigation or solve a problem.

• **Connecting** Students will make connections among mathematical concepts and procedures, and relate mathematical ideas to situations or phenomena drawn from other contexts.

• **Representing** Students will create basic representations of simple mathematical ideas.

• **Communicating** Students will communicate mathematical thinking orally, visually, and in writing, using everyday language, a basic mathematical vocabulary, and a variety of representations as well as observe basic mathematical conventions.</td>
</tr>
</table>

IMPROVISATIONAL ACTIVITY: SPACE WALK AND TABLEAU

Lesson: Painting Visualization

Grade level: fifth to ninth grade

Subject: visual arts

Time length for lesson: forty-five minutes if groups are predetermined and the students are given the paintings to recreate.

Maria Abbruzzese, a teacher from Ontario, Canada, authored this lesson plan.

Lesson Overview   The objective of the lesson is to have students familiarize themselves with a specific painting. Visualizing themselves in the painting allows them to understand mood, environment, depth, and character analysis in portraits.

This can be used as a ten-minute hook or introduction to critiquing a painting or to examining a painting as a class.

As a lesson, students can be placed into groups and given a painting to visualize and perform for their peers.

The students and teacher freeze during a Space Walk exercise.

Student Learning Objectives Students work collaboratively as a team to prepare and perform their visualization. They use drama elements of tableaux using various levels and staging, and improvisational skills.

Instructional Plan and Explanation of Learning Activities

Step One: Hook or introduction. Introduce the lesson by showing a painting to the class and then ask for volunteers to recreate the painting in front of the class.

Example: American realist artist Edward Hopper is a great choice for this lesson. Any one of these paintings would be sufficient:

Chop Suey (1929)

Nighthawks (1942)

Chair Car (1965)

Step Two: Explanation. Tell the students: "Today you will have an exciting opportunity to experience a painting and understand the artists' intentions for creating the painting by recreating the painting through drama." Discuss with students that by allowing themselves to visualize being in a painting they are able to better understand the painting and remember its elements.

Step Three: Techniques or skills to communicate:

Tableaux and levels

Space

Gestures

Body movement

Focus

Balance

Unity

Assessment Plan for Lesson The teacher should take anecdotal notes and observe the students for:

- Working collaboratively
- Respecting others
- Being focused and on task
- Offering ideas
- Demonstrating understanding

Subject: Visual Arts
Lesson: Painting Visualization

Grade Level	McREL Standards	Ontario Curriculum Ministry Expectations
5 6 7 8	3. Knows a range of subject matter, symbols, and potential ideas in the visual arts 4. Understands the visual arts in relation to history and cultures 5. Understands the characteristics and merits of one's own artwork and the artwork of others	• Students will describe their interpretation of a variety of art works, basing their interpretation on evidence from the works (especially on how an artist has used the elements of design to clarify meaning) and on their own knowledge and experience; students will use correctly vocabulary and art terminology associated with the specific expectations for this grade. • Students will explain their interpretation of a variety of art works, supporting it with examples of how the elements and some of the principles of design are used in the work; students will correctly use vocabulary and art terminology associated with the specific expectations for this grade. • Students will identify the principles of design (emphasis, rhythm, balance, unity, variety, proportion), and use them in ways appropriate for this grade in producing and responding to works of art; students will correctly use vocabulary and art terminology associated with the specific expectations for this grade. • Students will define the principles of design (emphasis, balance, rhythm, unity, variety, proportion), and use them in ways appropriate for this grade in producing and responding to works of art; students will correctly use vocabulary and art terminology associated with the specific expectations for this grade.

IMPROVISATIONAL ACTIVITY: STRING OF PEARLS

Lesson: String of Ideas

Grade level: fifth to eighth grade

Subject: extended response, mathematics

Time length for lesson: thirty to forty minutes

Lesson Overview This lesson was created by Bradley Berlage, a mathematics and English teacher in Chicago, Illinois. This activity can be used to enhance student understanding of mathematical concepts and how to apply them.

Student Learning Objectives The students discover a method of solving an equation by vocalizing their ideas and working as a group.

Instructional Plan and Explanation of Learning Activities

Step One: Students will are to the String of Pearls activity, usually first encountered during a previous class period.

The students listen carefully to the directions for
the improvisation exercise String of Pearls.

Step Two: Have the students create their own word problem by filling in the blanks to a problem similar to the one given here.

Sample Fill-in-the-Blank

(Student's name) wrote an essay of (number between 1 and 10 with decimal point; example 4.2) pages on the meaning of (noun). (Second student's name) wrote an essay on the same topic. Together, their essays were (larger number between 1 and 10 with decimal point) pages.

What is the equation you would use to find out how many pages (second student's name) wrote? Solve the equation.

Resulting Sample Word Problem

Jose wrote an essay of *3.7* pages on the meaning of *chocolate. Keira* wrote an essay on the same topic. Together, their essays were *6.3* pages. What is the equation you would use to find out how many pages *Keira* wrote? Solve the equation.

This word problem is used in the String of Pearls exercise.

Step Three: Limit the number of participants to ten students at the most. As each student gets up to add an idea to the String of Pearls, allow enough time for students to process what they need to do to create the equation. In addition, allow students to add statements that may be incorrect or ones that reflect their own insecurity about how to solve the problem. Having them know that the teacher is OK with their being unsure about their ideas helps build confidence in taking risks. This is part of the process they need to go through to discover the right answer.

Step Four: Play two rounds of the game. During each round, have one student write down what each person says as she creates the String of Ideas. After the game is over, write the ideas on poster paper for the students to see and review.

Step Five: Have the students respond to these questions, either in a group or on paper in their math journal:

• What was the most challenging aspect about this game?

• Did our response make sense?

- How was this different than trying to write just numbers to get our response or equation?

Assessment Plan for Lesson Facilitate a discussion about the exercise responding to the questions they wrote about in the math journal.

Additional Comments and Tips from the Teacher Being able to converse about mathematical concepts supports students as they prepare for testing that requires extended written response. It also allows students to process solving an equation as a group.

Subject: Mathematics
Lesson: String of Ideas

Grade Level	McREL Standards	Ontario Curriculum Ministry Expectations
5 6 7 8	1. Uses a variety of strategies in the problem-solving process 2. Understands and applies basic and advanced properties of the concepts of numbers 9. Understands the general nature and uses of mathematics	• **Problem solving** Students will develop, select, and apply problem-solving strategies as they pose and solve problems and conduct investigations, to help deepen their mathematical understanding. • **Reflecting** Students will demonstrate that they are reflecting on and monitoring their thinking to help clarify their understanding as they complete an investigation or solve a problem. • **Connecting** Students will make connections among mathematical concepts and procedures, and relate mathematical ideas to situations or phenomena drawn from other contexts. • **Communicating** Students will communicate mathematical thinking orally, visually, and in writing, using everyday language, a basic mathematical vocabulary, and a variety of representations as well as observe basic mathematical conventions.

IMPROVISATIONAL ACTIVITY: TABLEAU ACTIVITY
Lesson: Tableau Activity for Analytic Geometry

Grade level: sixth to eighth grade

Subject: mathematics

Time length for lesson: fifty to sixty minutes. May be suitable for two class periods.

Tenth grade mathematics teacher Diane E. Vivian of Ontario, Canada, created this lesson. Although it was created for a tenth grade geometry class, it is included because it demonstrates how to teach abstract mathematical concepts with improvisation exercises.

Lesson Overview   This is a review activity for analytic geometry.

Student Learning Objectives   The students identify the necessary requirements to determine special lines in a triangle, centers of a triangle, and geometric figures.

The students reinforce skills and definitions that they have already learned as well as the skills to break down a problem into multiple steps.

Instructional Plan and Explanation of Learning Activities

Step One: Cards are made up ahead of time (from Handout Number 1) with these words:

Median	Rhombus
Altitude	Trapezoid
Perpendicular bisector	Square
Orthocenter	Rectangle
Centroid	Kite
Circumcenter	Parallelogram

The students review geometry terminology for about five to ten minutes.

Step Two: Introduce activity. Explain the nature of the activity: the students need to quickly assess how they should display their term as a tableau and set up without talking. Explain that the students observing are required to complete the chart regarding the tableau that has been displayed. This should take about five to ten minutes.

Step Three: Students are then given a card that they have about a minute to decide how to act out; and then the rest of the class needs to write down their guess as well as all the reasons they used to determine their guess.

Each group takes approximately three to five minutes to display its tableau. There should be some time for each student observing to complete the chart for each tableau (five minutes times ten to twelve cards equals fifty to sixty minutes).

Step Four: Discuss in a large group how the justifications furnish the means for determining which formula(s) to use to:

- Find the equation of a median
- Find the equation of an altitude
- Find the equation of a perpendicular bisector
- Find the coordinates of the orthocenter
- Find the coordinates of the centroid
- Find the coordinates of the circumcenter
- Justify that a figure is a rhombus
- Justify that a figure is a square
- Justify that a figure is a kite
- Justify that a figure is a parallelogram
- Justify that a figure is a trapezoid
- Justify that a figure is a rectangle

Assessment Plan for Lesson   Using the completed Handout Number 2, the teacher conducts a large-group discussion that specifically focuses on the last column, "Justifications for Guess," to determine the students' growing understanding of the key concepts from this lesson.

Handout Number 1: Tableau Activity for Analytic Geometry

Median	Perpendicular bisector
Altitude	Median
Orthocenter	Circumcenter
Rhombus	Trapezoid
Square	Rectangle
Parallelogram	Kite

Handout Number 2: Tableau Activity For Analytic Geometry

Name _____

Date _____

Analytic Geometry: Tableau Activity

Group No.	Activity No.	Guess	Justifications for Guess
(Example:) 1	1	Median of a triangle	The line from Bart, who was the vertex, went to the midpoint of the side formed by Lisa and Maggie.

Subject: Mathematics
Lesson: Tableau Activity for Analytic Geometry

Grade Level	McREL Standards	Ontario Curriculum Ministry Expectations
6	**Mathematics standards** 5. Understands and applies basic and advanced properties of the concepts of geometry 9. Understands the general nature and uses of mathematics	• **Reflecting** Students will demonstrate that they are reflecting on and monitoring their thinking to help clarify their understanding as they complete an investigation or solve a problem. • **Connecting** Students will make connections among mathematical concepts and procedures, and relate mathematical ideas to situations or phenomena drawn from other contexts. • **Representing** Students will create basic representations of simple mathematical ideas. • **Communicating** Students will communicate mathematical thinking orally, visually, and in writing, using everyday language, a basic mathematical vocabulary, and a variety of representations as well as observe basic mathematical conventions.

IMPROVISATIONAL ACTIVITY: TABLEAU ACTIVITY

Lesson: Picture Book Tableau

Grade level: third grade

Subject: reading and language arts

Time length for lesson: forty minutes

Third grade teacher Sara Spencer from Ontario, Canada, created this lesson.

Lesson Overview   Here are the lesson objectives:

- To read a new picture book
- To discuss how the title character from *Clancy the Courageous Cow* is different from the rest of his herd.
- To understand the importance of difference.

Instructional Plan and Explanation of Learning Activities

Step One: The teacher conducts a read-aloud of a new picture book to the class. I read *Clancy the Courageous Cow* by Lachie Hume to the class, asking questions along the way and allowing for think, pair, and share time. This book focuses on Clancy's individuality and two herds of cows and their prejudices toward each other.

I asked the class if they knew what improv meant. One student suggested it meant "improvisitation." We remind each other about being a community in the classroom where we support and encourage each other to be successful.

Step Two: The students are divided into groups of three or four students by the teacher to present a "secret" tableau scene to their classmates.

Step Three: The students are given about ten minutes to rehearse the secret tableau scene in order to present it to the rest of the class. As the students rehearse the tableau scenes, it is important for the teacher to circulate among the groups to ensure that there is no duplication of topics and to assist the students with their dramatic representations.

Step Four: The students present their tableau scenes, and the audience members are given the opportunity to guess the scene from the picture book and offer positive feedback and suggestions for improvement. The teacher may model phrases such as "I like ——— in the scene." Or "I could understand the main idea of the scene because the actors did ———." The students are reminded by their teacher to provide supportive and positive comments to their classmates.

Step Five: Once all of the scenes are performed, the students can respond orally or in a journal to these questions:

- What did you learn from creating your tableau scene?
- Why is this important?
- How did it contribute to your understanding of the story?

Assessment Plan for Lesson   After each group presents its tableau, audience members are given an opportunity to guess the scene, and give positive feedback and suggestions for improvement.

Additional Comments and Tips from the Teacher   Although not necessary, it's always helpful to have a variety of costumes and props that the students can use for their tableau scenes.

The students enjoy this activity, and they can do it several times a year.

Subject: Reading and Language Arts Lesson: Picture Book Tableau		
Grade Level	**McREL Standards**	**Ontario Curriculum Ministry Expectations**
3	4. Gathers and uses information for research purposes 5. Uses the general skills and strategies of the reading process 8. Uses listening and speaking strategies for different purposes	**3.** Create a variety of media texts for different purposes and audiences, using appropriate forms, conventions, and techniques

IMPROVISATIONAL ACTIVITY: TABLEAU ACTIVITY

Lesson: In-Class Field Trip—Using Tableaux to Explore the Role of Perception in Communication

Grade level: seventh to eighth grade
Subject: language arts
Time length for lesson: fifty minutes

Diane Walker, a high school teacher from Normal, Illinois, created this lesson.

Lesson Overview   Students explore the role of perception in the communication process. They specifically examine how messages can change based on the perceptions of the sender and receiver.

Instructional Plan and Explanation of Learning Activities   This lesson is used in a tenth grade-level, one-semester Oral Communication course. It is adaptable to a variety of grade levels and concepts. Prior to the In-Class Field Trip lesson, the significance of communication, the communication process, and communication models have been covered in previous lessons.

Learning Activities

Step One: At the beginning of class, the teacher announces to the class the "good news" and the "bad news. " The good news is that the class is going on a field trip (cheers!). The bad news is that the field trip is virtual, meaning they will not have to leave the classroom (boos!).

Step Two: The term *perception* is introduced and defined. It is noted that an understanding of perception and its role in communication is the key to becoming effective, skilled communicators.

Step Three: Students are asked to answer these questions:

• You get to sleep in on Saturdays. What time do you get up?

• You had a good dinner. What would this include?

• You are doing OK in school. What grades are you getting?

From these responses, it is noted that because of varied fields of experience humans perceive messages differently.

Step Four: To further explore this concept, the teacher introduces the field trip to the "Museum of Human Modern Art." The most popular exhibit allows visitors to create their own masterpieces—using *themselves* as the medium!

Step Five: The teacher volunteers to be the first artist and creates a "masterpiece" by maneuvering a few students into an abstract tableau.

Step Six: All other students are asked to write a title for this piece of art.

Step Seven: Subsequent artists are selected among student volunteers. Each student artist arranges a group of peers into an abstract tableau. Students continue to write titles for each tableau. This is repeated four to five times depending on student engagement.

Step Eight: Digital pictures are taken of each tableau.

Step Nine: After all the exhibits have been created, the pictures can be projected via LCD projector. Student-generated titles for each tableau are compared.

Step Ten: Similarities and differences in titles are identified and discussed. Reasons for varied titles are identified. The relationship between perception and communication is discussed.

Step Eleven: The definition of perception is reviewed and students are asked, on the basis of what they discovered during the field trip, why an understanding of perception and its role in communication is imperative to developing effective communication skills.

Assessment Plan for Lesson   Assessment is informal. It is through the post-activity discussion that the teacher determines if objectives have been met. These objectives are reviewed and reinforced throughout the rest of the semester course as students analyze and create varied messages.

Additional Comments from the Teacher   The set induction for this lesson (announcement of field trip) is presented in an exaggerated tone, parodying an elementary setting. It is a fun way to engage the students. The teacher, throughout this lesson, sustains a playful tone, encouraging students to relax and play as they create their masterpieces.

Use of the digital camera is optional. Students can share and discuss their titles as each tableau is presented. A camera keeps students from having to stay in the frozen tableau for long, allowing extended discussion.

Traditionally, actors create tableaux through a process of ensemble work. In this case, only one student/actor shapes the tableau. This works well for students who are tentative about being in front of the class and engaging in improvisation. In this lesson, someone else puts the student into the tableau, minimizing the risk factor. Ultimately, students may feel comfortable enough to be encouraged to "enter into" a tableau as it is being created.

Subject: Language Arts
Lesson: In-Class Field Trip: Using Tableaux to Explore the Role of Perception in Communication

Grade Level	McREL Standards	Ontario Curriculum Ministry Expectations
7 8	8. Uses listening and speaking strategies for various purposes 10. Understands the characteristics and components of the media	• **Reflecting** Students will demonstrate that they are reflecting on and monitoring their thinking to help clarify their understanding as they complete an investigation or solve a problem. • **Connecting** Students will make connections among mathematical concepts and procedures, and relate mathematical ideas to situations or phenomena drawn from other contexts. • **Representing** Students will create basic representations of simple mathematical ideas. • **Communicating** Students will communicate mathematical thinking orally, visually, and in writing, using everyday language, a basic mathematical vocabulary, and a variety of representations as well as observe basic mathematical conventions.

IMPROVISATIONAL ACTIVITY: THROWING LIGHT

Lesson: Throwing Math Light

Grade level: fourth to eighth grade
Subject: mathematics concept review
Time length for lesson: thirty minutes

This lesson was created by Bradley Berlage, a mathematics and English teacher in Chicago.

Lesson Overview This activity can be used prior to a quiz or test to assist students in developing a stronger understanding of the material.

Student Learning Objectives The students communicate using mathematical concepts and gain deeper understanding of mathematical concepts and how to apply them through participating in this improvisational exercise.

Instructional Plan and Explanation of Learning Activities

Step One: Students are introduced to the Throwing Light activity, usually first encountered during a previous class period.

Step Two: Teacher prepares a list of mathematical concepts that he or she wants the students to become familiar with through review. These concepts are placed on the walls around the classroom as they are introduced.

For example, if the class has been analyzing data using graphs, the concepts listed might include bar graphs, line graphs, tables, and so on.

If the class has been covering number sense, it might include percentages, fractions, and decimals.

Step Three: The teacher reminds the students of the Throwing Light exercise they have previously done and introduces the Throwing Math Light exercise with a simple example that she starts. For example, if the topic is fractions, the conversation might include these topics:

- I always get confused when I have to add them, especially if the bottoms are different.

- I usually use them when I have to split up stuff, like food I may be making, or when I need to see if I have enough money to buy a soda.

- My brother and I usually have to split stuff too, so we usually use them for that.

Step Four: Have students take turns introducing a topic. Allow the students to ask the teacher if they are concerned about their topic.

Assessment Plan Play four rounds of the game, and then have the students respond to these questions, either in a group or on paper in their math journals:

- How did you know what they were talking about? When did you know it?
- Did anyone join in the conversation without knowing what the topic was?
- Could we tell when someone didn't know or was wrong about what the topic was? How could we tell?

Additional Comments and Tips from the Teacher Many people may feel that using math concepts with improvisation is not valuable, but it gives students the opportunity to converse and interact with mathematics outside of textbooks or worksheets. In addition, once students are able to discuss and converse about mathematics, their ability to apply the mathematical concepts increases. Time must also be allowed for students to vocalize their frustration about mathematics or lack of understanding about math into the exercises. With time and repetitive application of these improvisation activities, you will find that students are able to apply these concepts and as a result build their own sense of self-efficacy with the topic at hand.

Subject: Mathematics
Lesson: Throwing Math Light

Grade Level	McREL Standards	Ontario Curriculum Ministry Expectations
4 5 6 7 8	1. Uses a variety of strategies in the problem-solving process 9. Understands the general nature and uses of mathematics	• **Reflecting** Students will demonstrate that they are reflecting on and monitoring their thinking to help clarify their understanding as they complete an investigation or solve a problem. • **Connecting** Students will make connections among mathematical concepts and procedures, and relate mathematical ideas to situations or phenomena drawn from other contexts. • **Communicating** Students will communicate mathematical thinking orally, visually, and in writing, using everyday language, a basic mathematical vocabulary, and a variety of representations as well as observe basic mathematical conventions.

Engaging Students in Learning

In a time when teachers feel extraordinary pressure to teach to specific standardized assessments, we need to redirect ourselves to what good teaching and learning are about. Good teaching focuses on creating experiences that engage students in authentic learning. The fine arts, visual arts, music, and drama are especially effective tools for creating experiences of this kind. Unfortunately, in too many school districts the arts have fallen victim to budget cuts. They have been conspicuously omitted from the schedule in response to the call that more time is needed to teach the core subjects: reading, math, social studies, and science. Policymakers fail to realize the critical need for schools to teach art forms *because these experiences help students learn.* It is through students' participation in the artistic process—or authoring—that they develop critical thinking skills that are the catalyst for a greater and broader learning experience.

When students engage in an artistic discipline such as improvisation and are able to have authoring experiences, they take what they know and reshape it in ways that are personally meaningful and original. This is how we develop original thinkers and leaders for our democracy. Teaching and learning is not a lockstep process; it is a fluid and ever-changing one. Montessori and Spolin shared this philosophy, and the Second City educational programs have fostered it through teacher and classroom relationships.

AUTHENTIC AND ENGAGED LEARNING

We have presented evidence that our assertions are correct. In Chapter Two, we examined the connections between improvisation and engaged and authentic learning through the experience of creating original texts that are personal, meaningful, and specific for individual groups of students. We know that students who engage in improvisation activities in the classroom develop skills in listening, following directions, focus, oral communication, team building, empathy, self-awareness, self-confidence, critical and creative problem solving, and idea generation. Of course, all of these skills are necessary for engaged, authentic, and motivating learning experiences.

We know that the classroom must be interactive and that learning activities are a partnership between the classroom teacher and the students. This focus must be paramount at a time when educational initiatives and school structures are not always conducive to this model. As educators, we must band together and implement innovative pedagogies, such as improvisation, in the classroom. We need innovative pedagogies in our classrooms because they create opportunities for students to grow intellectually and emotionally as they speculate, reason, and predict.

In addition to our cry to create innovative, active, and engaging learning environments, we must remind ourselves of this increased need as our classrooms become increasingly diverse. As we examined in Chapter Two, our students with special needs have much to gain from pedagogical activities such as improvisation. Our work in schools has demonstrated that these students benefit tremendously from greater opportunity for a meaningful context for collaboration and negotiation. Engaging all students in teaching and learning activities such as improvisation transcends these barriers. Isn't this an essential component for the education of members of our democratic society? John Dewey (1966), the famous American educational philosopher, would concur.

In addition to the authentic and engaging learning experiences that improvisation promotes, there is also evidence from recent brain research supporting the assertion that children learn better when they are exposed to a variety of educational experiences. Improvisation is a dynamic and malleable learning experience where students develop skills and competency in all content areas.

THE LITERACY CONNECTION

We examined the benefits of improvisation for instruction of all content areas, and the connections to literacy are especially important to revisit. As we revealed in Chapter Three, improvisation activities and literacy are directly linked. The skill sets that a student applies in literacy, prediction, sequencing, vocabulary building, inferencing, and reflection are all used in improvisation exercises. A key difference is that in improvisation a student is practicing these skills in an active and engaging manner. Imagine the impact this could have on a kinesthetic learner.

SOME FINAL THOUGHTS

At a time when standardized test scores and other external pressures weigh heavily on our educational system, we must be careful about shortsightedness. Is education merely about meeting external mandates, at the sacrifice of the arts

and other important areas of the school curriculum? We argue that improvisation as a pedagogical strategy is the key to unlocking a student's connection to the "hard" subjects of mathematics, reading, writing, science, and social studies. Now we come full circle to our original assertion: that *play and education are inextricably linked.*

Reference
Dewey, J. (1966). *The child and the curriculum.* Chicago: University of Chicago Press.

INDEX

O

CPSIA information can be obtained at www.ICGtesting.com
Printed in the USA
BVOW10n0346220715

409589BV00006B/15/P